Noble Tennis:
The Wisdom of Sport

By
Tony Roth

NOBLE TENNIS
THE WISDOM OF SPORT

Noble Tennis: The Wisdom of Sport
©2000 by A.D. Roth

All rights reserved. No part of this publication may be reproduced or transmitted in any form or by any means, electronic or mechanical, including photocopying, recording, or information storage and retrieval without permission in writing from the published.

Canadian Cataloguing in Publication Data
Roth, A.D. 1970

Noble Tennis: The Wisdom of Sport
ISBN 0-9688139-0-9

1. Sports - Psychological aspects.
2. Sports – Philosophy.
3. Tennis - Psychological aspects.
I. Title

GV1002.9.P57R68 1999 796'.01 C99-901001-8

Second Publishing in 2000 by
Après Fou Publishing
R.R. 2 Perth Road, Kingston, Ontario, Canada K0H 2L0
www.apresfou.com

Cover Photo-Illustration and Book Design
Stone and Associates - Designers
www-stone-and-associates.com

Printed and bound in Canada

NOBLE TENNIS
THE WISDOM OF SPORT

Table of Contents

Opening Volleys
    Welcome **8**
    Genesis **10**
    Statement of Intent **12**
    The Game... **13**
    A Thought Experiment...................... **16**
    Defining Terms..................................... **18**
Chapter One: Enthusiasm............................ **19**
Chapter Two: Serenity................................. **37**
Chapter Three: Patience............................. **53**
Chapter Four: Concentration..................... **67**
Chapter Five: Understanding Fear............ **77**
Chapter Six: Fearlessness.......................... **87**
Chapter Seven: The Inner Life................. **101**
Chapter Eight: Physical Cooperation....... **117**
Chapter Nine: Odds and Ends.................. **133**
Chapter Ten: The Wisdom of Sport **151**
A Concluding Analogy................................ **157**
Appendices
#1: The Qualitative Approach:
    A Case Study **162**
#2: Competition and Cooperation:
    The Connection? **166**
#3: The Dignity of Sport **169**
Try This! Summary **172**

NOBLE TENNIS
THE WISDOM OF SPORT

Forward
by Pierre Lamarche

Tony Roth was a gifted child when he walked into the All-Canadian Tennis Academy in London, Ontario in the 1980's. The Academy, the first of its kind in Canada, fostered excellence in youngsters. The leadership of the Academy was provided by individuals such as Ven Sinclair, a many times World Champion and Harry Fauquier a ten time Davis Cup player for Canada. The day to day guidance of the youngsters was the responsibility of individuals such as World Squash Champion Mac Kerim and many times senior World Tennis Champion, Lorne Main This environment developed the leaders, as players and administrators, of Canadian Tennis for the 1990 decade. The environment also provided a pool of talented people who achieved excellence in other areas of life. Tony Roth emerged from this creative and inspirational environment, as is reflected in his new book, NOBLE TENNIS: THE WISDOM OF SPORT.

It is not a surprise that Tony, with his background as a player and a student of philosophy, would create a practical work that is destined to change and improve greatly the way in which we assist the development of our youth through sport. Tennis teaching was in the dark ages till the late 1980's when a systematic approach was developed to provide coaches with tools for a more holistic approach to player development. Revolutionary teaching methods in the tactical/technical area, pioneered by Canadian teaching guru Louis Cayer, complemented detailed work provided by former German National Coach Richard Schornborn in the physical development component. The area of mental skills was addressed through works in the area of sport psychology championed by such individuals as world renowned James Loehr

NOBLE TENNIS
THE WISDOM OF SPORT

of the US. However, this seemingly holistic approach lacked several major components: an overall philosophy of sport, personal development of the athlete, and a real understanding of the deeper sources of "the zone." NOBLE TENNIS THE WISDOM OF SPORT addresses these crucial areas in a clear and engaging way.

Sport psychology has brought much insight on how to cope with problems created by stress in competitive sport. Most of the solutions are formulas for dealing with specific problems through a responsive behaviour. NOBLE TENNIS: THE WISDOM OF SPORT goes a big step further: it deals with developing those qualities that provide us with the ability to eliminate problems, rather than trying to manage them. Through his discussions on topics such as fearlessness, patience and concentration, Tony Roth has presented a paradigm shift in athletics. At a time when new age concepts reflect Mankind's search for better ways to deal with traditional problems, NOBLE TENNIS: THE WISDOM OF SPORT provides us with the ideas and information we need to really reap the rewards of sport, at the levels of personal development and athletic performance.

One of the most successful coaches in Canadian history, **Pierre Lamarche** *is currently Director of the Ace Tennis Academy in Burlington, Ontario. He was the Team Leader at the 1996 Olympic Games in Atlanta, and is a former captain of Federation Cup and Davis Cup Teams.*

NOBLE TENNIS
THE WISDOM OF SPORT

O seeker,

Rely on nothing

until you Want nothing

The Dhammapada

Opening Volleys

NOBLE TENNIS
THE WISDOM OF SPORT

Welcome

If sport is wisdom,
And wisdom is grace,
Then you, my friend,
Are in the right place.

You search for a thing
Beyond glitz and show,
A better, cleaner,
Higher place to go.

Then come for a ride,
A ponder, a peek,
Come if you know
The meaning of "seek."

A way does exist,
Please have no fear,
The answers, you'll find,
Will simply appear.

They tell us that sport
Is a way to survive,
But what about purpose -
To where should we strive?

They tell us the game's
A behavioral tool,
But what if we want
To be nobody's fool?

They say all the work
Is good in the end,
It brings to us fame,
And money to spend;

They say old ambition's
A wonderful sight,
In spite of the fact
It brings such a fright.

Enough with this twaddle,
Enough with dance,
Philosophy speaks,
And it takes a new stance.

Play is natural,
Striving is fun,
Amongst our instincts,
One is called "run."

NOBLE TENNIS
THE WISDOM OF SPORT

The wisdom of sport
Is the path to what's great,
And the way there is ethics -
It's narrow and straight.

Or, should I say,
Let us all find the zone,
I offer a way -
For keeps, not on loan.

Qualities, virtues,
That is the path,
So come take the plunge,
Who cares if they laugh!

Coaches, parents,
Players too,
All are invited,
The words are for you.

Today we all say,
"Hooray for ability,"
But the path to the zone
Is the way of nobility.

That is the insight
For us to explore,
And this, I daresay,
Will not be a bore.

So welcome, welcome,
And welcome once more,
For dignity's sake,
Let's aim-shoot-and-score!

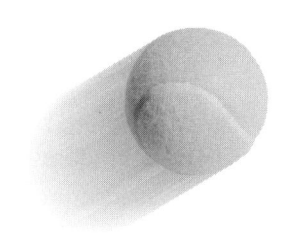

NOBLE TENNIS
THE WISDOM OF SPORT

Genesis

Picture, if you will, a fifteen year old boy, lying on his bed at 11:30 p.m. and debating over whether to award himself a 7.0 or a 7.2 out of 10 under the category of "patience." Each day he rates himself in thirty such categories - almost all of which deal with attitudes, virtues and qualities - and records his findings on a graph. Did he think before he spoke? Was he mean and sarcastic, or was he kind? Did he apply one hundred per cent effort to his work, whatever it was? Did he keep his things neat and tidy? Did he bite his nails, or was he calm and disciplined?

Who is this boy? It's me, Tony Roth.

Where is he? At the All-Canadain Tennis Academy in London, Ontario.

What, exactly, is he doing? A refined version of the goal-setting program that was instituted during his second year at the academy (1985-86). He's taken what was presented and interpreted almost exclusively in terms of rankings and physical-technical capacities, and transformed it into an ethical and qualitative enterprise.

Why is he doing this? At the time, he isn't fully aware of the meaning and significance of his endeavors. He doesn't yet realize their implications in terms of philosophy, psychology and methods of training; nor has he synthesized the many qualities down to the five indispensables of enthusiasm, serenity, patience, concentration and fearlessness. However, he is innately aware of

NOBLE 🎾 TENNIS
THE WISDOM OF SPORT

two crucial things: first, that the ultimate value of the athletic enterprise is in the growth and development of human beings, *as human beings*, not just as players; and second, that there's an intimate connection between how the game is played, and who plays it - between the qualities of the person and the "performance" of the player.

In short, this boy knows that if he is patience, if that becomes a feature of who he is, and not just a behavioral or temporary overlay, then his tennis will benefit; and, conversely, and more importantly, if tennis helps him to become patience, he, the human being, and everyone who knows him, benefits. In this way, he's breaking down the false barriers between on and off-court training, between the psychological and the physical, the inner and the outer, the ethical and the competitive, the life of "the person" and the life of "the player." This blending, this unifying and harmonizing, is wisdom. When it's achieved through athletics, we may call it *the wisdom of sport*.

NOBLE TENNIS
THE WISDOM OF SPORT

Statement of Intent

The purpose of this book is to steer the ship of sport in a new direction. Chiefly, I'm concerned with how sport can aid in the growth and development of human beings, as human beings. I see this as the fundamental task of every athletic endeavour. What's offered here is not a system True, I have furnished many hints and tips, as well as illustrative and anecdotal stories (most of which come from the sport of tennis, which is where I am most familiar), but there will be no "do this, then do this, then do this." Instead I make available an *approach* to sport that releases creativity and channels it along harmless, constructive lines. This "qualitative approach" solves the riddle of "the zone" - that mysterious phenomenon where greatness flows naturally from every fibre of our being, and it paves the way for an ethical and spiritual regeneration of sport. Thus, this book can't be pigeon-holed. It is philosophy, psychology and physical training, synthesized into a whole by the guiding light of nobility and the power of virtue. I suggest that players and coaches who place their emphasis on the release of ennobling and enabling qualities have discovered the meaning and significance of sport. They have escaped from the tedium of mechanics for mechanics' sake, the strictly quantitative dimension; they have entered a realm of beauty, and limitless possibilities.

The Game

The time has come to discover the game.

The game -

Not the rules, not the brain, not the net loss and gain,
But the game-in-itself,
The underlying thing,
What does it do, what does it bring?

Think about sport - is it wholesome and good?
Does it serve Man, as it can-must-and-should?
Does it evoke what is noble and fine?
Or does it fall short of this every darn time?

Let me be clear,
We're missing the mark,
We're groping around,
Lost in the dark.

We jump, we bound,
We run 'round the bend,
But the question remains -
To what end?

NOBLE 🎾 TENNIS
THE WISDOM OF SPORT

To answer this query,
We must stop and think;
We must go to wisdom,
And from its cup - drink.

The wisdom of sport
Is refinement of life,
The movement to harmony
From conflict and strife.

Today we revel
In aims and goals -
What dusty closets!
What rocky shoals!

There's a bigger pattern,
A bigger way;
Let nature speak,
Let nature play!

Are you attracted,
Are you intrigued;
If you are a warrior,
Come, you'll be pleased.

NOBLE TENNIS
THE WISDOM OF SPORT

Let us engage
In noble battle:
Knowledge and truth
Versus uninformed prattle!

It's one or the other,
The solution is here:
Discover serenity,
Abolish fear.

Then, in the moment,
You are the zone;
The game is discovered,
Its meaning is known.

This is our task,
This is our fate;
All things considered,
Isn't it great?

NOBLE TENNIS
THE WISDOM OF SPORT

A Thought Experiment

Let's imagine there was a great world conference, and all the people, by international referendum, agreed to rid the world of violence and conflict of every kind. Imagine we finally became completely and utterly dissatisfied with divisiveness, separateness and brutality; that we became aware of the results of these things - war, conflict, suffering, hate, fear, misery - and that we really and truly said "that's enough, let's move on."

Now let me pose this question - would sport have any place in such a new world? The answer, for the most part, is no. At least, that's the answer if we accept the current way of thinking about it, speaking about it, teaching it and playing it. Sport, like everything else in the world right now, is permeated by violence. Is it not true that sport and conflict are presently seen as one and the same thing? An athletic contest is "a battle," a war, a competition between separate teams or individuals, and the key requirement for victory is aggression, of one sort or another. Indeed, our whole language is permeated with conflict: players must "develop a weapon," they must "exploit weaknesses," they must "throw bombs" and hit "attacking shots."

Seeing this violence in sport, and seeing the chaos and misery that violence spreads in the world, we are led to this question - is it possible to approach sport in a completely non-violent, non-conflictual way? The answer, thankfully, is yes. In fact, as we'll see, the non-violent approach to sport is by far the most natural, most intelligent, most effective one. The key to this approach is contained in one word – *harmony*. Harmony involves allowing

NOBLE TENNIS
THE WISDOM OF SPORT

things to work together; it involves cooperation, and this means that every instrument in the symphony of sport will fulfill its rightful function. Those elements whose only function is to produce divisiveness and discord will be shed, left behind as irrelevant and out-dated. This is very sensible, for harmony is the key to happiness and effectiveness: harmony of mind and body; harmony between players, coaches and parents; harmony in all things and at all times. This is the vision. Harmony can become the keynote of sport at all levels – philosophical, psychological, physical, tactical and technical. It can become the theme of playing, coaching and parenting. Competitions can lose their character as sites of conflict, gamesmanship, grimness and violence. They can become joyous events whose theme is perfectment and mutual striving. The purpose of this book is to demonstrate how this is so, and to begin the work of re-orientating our thoughts and methods along harmonious lines.

Defining Terms

Noble
From the Latin *noscere;* to perceive or understand as fact or truth with clearness and certainty; admirable in dignity of conception, or in the manner of expression, execution or composition; of an admirably high quality.

Wisdom
The faculty to discern right and truth and to act accordingly.

Philosophy
The love or pursuit of wisdom; a system of principles for guidance in practical affairs.

Ethics
An assemblage of guidelines for effecting the self-transformation that enables the world to be experienced in a new way.*

Taken from Huston Smith's Beyond the Post-Modern Mind (Wheaton, Illinois, USA: Quest, Theosophical Publishing House, 1989, p.73).

NOBLE TENNIS
THE WISDOM OF SPORT

CHAPTER ONE
Enthusiasm

The task of the Athlete.
The keynote of sport is harmony. What does this mean? Simply, it means the task of the athlete is to unify or bring together various qualities and actions. This applies in the technical and physical sense: power must be united with finesse, and dynamic speed with composed balance. It also applies in the psychological sense. The most important thing is to combine enthusiasm and serenity, or calmness. So let us examine these crucial attributes, beginning with enthusiasm.

A Confucian credo.
It was said of Confucius, the great Eastern sage, that he never accepted a student who wasn't literally "bubbling over" with enthusiasm. That was a great piece of wisdom. Enthusiasm is the first key to greatness.

Defining Enthusiasm

A centrifugal dynamo.
Technically speaking, enthusiasm can be defined as an outgoing or centrifugal energy. Enthusiasm breeds motion; it proceeds towards the object of interest; it advances relentlessly!

It's everywhere!
There are countless expressions of enthusiasm, ranging all the way from simple curiosity to contrived ambitions and fantasies. Indeed, where there is life, there is also enthusiasm. However, the *intensity and quality* of that enthusiasm covers an immense range. In its purest and most beneficial form, enthusiasm is expressed as innocent or natural love. The player who truly "loves the game" is attracted to it in the same way that iron filings are attracted to a magnet - spontaneously, naturally and powerfully.

If this initial attraction is followed, if we let it move us, then we are swept into a current of striving and learning that is completely beneficial.

The Enthusiast

The "nature" of enthusiasm.

Pure, natural enthusiasm can't be artificially generated. You can't whip it up through ambition, with its accompanying emotions and images of grandeur. Enthusiasm is there; it's within you. It brings with it a sense of lightness, intelligent flow and rhythm. You cannot create enthusiasm, any more than you can create life. What you can do is recognize it, affirm it, participate in it, cooperate with it, enhance it, and, in general, honor it.

Enthusiasm repels tyranny!

Usually, enthusiasts have no concept of themselves as enthusiastic. When you stop and say, "I am enthusiastic, and I will stay this way," the enthusiasm becomes something you want to possess and repeat. You try to dominate and package enthusiasm, making it the servant of your "goals"; you have an ambition to be enthusiastic, an image of yourself that you try to manipulate into existence. In this there is the fear of failure, and enthusiasm loses its purity; the *flow* is interrupted, and everything becomes a struggle, rather than an adventure. The wise athlete learns that life-enthusiasm contains an intelligence, a capacity for guidance along life-enhancing lines, that far outstrips that of our little, calculating, manipulating self. In the flow of enthusiasm, our potential and our destiny naturally unfold. Thus, the enthusiast is the enthusiasm. Our responsibility is to notice and reject that which negates enthusiasm. The enthusiasm itself cannot be coerced into existence.

The flow of enthusiasm.

The athlete who truly loves their sport doesn't feel the need to prop up their attraction with artificial goals and ambitions. Results and achievements are *effects* of the quality and consistency of our actions. Such quality and consistency is guaranteed by the accumulations of experience and knowledge that enthusiasm always brings about. When the simplicity of love is combined with grasping, personal desires, enthusiasm is expressed in the form of ambition, greed and "competitiveness." Now apart from their dubious stature as virtues, these modifications of enthusiasm are inherently dangerous. Each of them is based in the sentiment called "I want." This, in turn, carries the possibility of failure (i.e. I wanted, but I didn't get). This possibility of failure produces fear, and fear is the great breeder of misery, misbehaviour and, ironically, failure. Thus, we must maintain the purity of our enthusiasm, and simple love must be the only thing that motivates our actions. Play and teach within the flow of joyous enthusiasm, thereby banishing fear. All the rest will follow. This paragraph, if pondered and applied, contains a revolution.

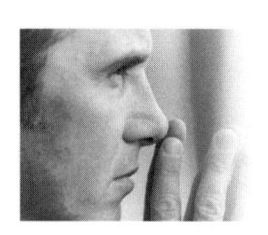

Try This!

When scouting, look for people who are preoccupied with their sport in the absence of any coercion or outward incentives. For instance, the young tennis player: when faced with a choice, do they watch tennis? When all the courts at the club are booked, do they sneak into a squash court and play? Do they hit against the wall? Do they read tennis books and magazines? These are important indicators, which should be considered by parents as well as coaches. We must learn the difference between fleeting curiosity and deep enthusiasm.

Impure enthusiasm.

When actions are spurred on by fear we can call it "impure enthusiasm." Indeed, the heated efforts that follow on the heels of ambition and greed serve to pervert the athletic endeavor. Under the influence of fear, sport takes to itself a savage and brutal tone. Thus, I protest against the glorification of the adrenal glands within the realm of sport! As if tennis bears any relation to issues of physical survival! The keynotes of sport, as a noble enterprise, are beauty, grace, power and harmony; love, not fear, is its motivating impulse, and the instincts that relate to brute survival are lost in the light of human striving and artistic expression.

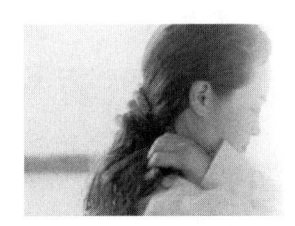

Try This!

Beware of the many pitfalls that can sap the purity of enthusiasm. At tournaments, for instance, stand aloof from the incessant speculation over results, rankings, etc. The sport is the source of joy, and the aim is to participate fully in the playing. Everything else is secondary, and follows naturally from this innocent absorption.

The noble amateur.

The pure enthusiast is a proponent of the amateur approach to sport. The word amateur comes from the Latin roots "*amator*" - lover, and "*amare*" - love. Thus, anyone who isn't an amateur is playing, or coaching, for something other than love. This is both unwholesome and inefficient, not to mention irrational! Does this mean that money and rankings, and everything associated with professional sport should be abandoned, or abolished? No, not necessarily. Amateurism is essentially a state of mind, or a condition of being. A committed amateur, or a pure enthusiast, can regard money, for instance, as an incidental effect of their love and striving, and they will receive it in this spirit. The problem, of course, is when money *replaces* love as the motivating impulse for the activity, and this seems to happen almost all the time. Yes, the purity of enthusiasm can be maintained, but how often is it?

Try This!

Avoid the temptation to consider athletics as an "investment" – that is, something from which some material or status-related benefit will come. These things may occur, but when these motivations replace enthusiasm, the situation is destructive and unwholesome. Parents, do you really wish to think of your children as corporations, and you a shareholder? Do you want to drive your child, like investors drive corporations, to seek material profit at any cost, knowing that 'failure' will result in withdrawn support? Are you content being a fear-monger? Psychological well-being is the top priority. All the rest follows. Look for pure enthusiasm, and work with it. Applying this hint may require some inward de-programming. Observe your thoughts, words and deeds, and substitute vital, joyous enthusiasm for grasping, smothering desires.

Effects of Enthusiasm

Commitment.
Commitment, or sustained attention and striving, is a *natural* effect of enthusiasm; and pure commitment is very powerful. As W.H. Murray says,

The moment one definitely commits oneself,
then providence moves too.
All sorts of things occur to help one
that would otherwise never have occurred.
A whole stream of events issue from the decision,
raising in one's favor all manner of unforeseen incidents
and meetings and material assistance,
which no man could have dreamt would come his way.
I have learned a deep respect for one of Goethe's couplets:
Whatever you can do, or dream you can,
begin it.
Boldness has genius, power and magic in it.

The validity of these statements has been a part of my own experience. Pure enthusiasm contains a mysterious intelligence, and phrases like "a current of striving and learning" aren't just metaphorical, or poetic; they are factual.

Energy, attention and "heroism."
The psychological and physiological effects of pure enthusiasm are quite astonishing. It's like being connected to a source of energy that's literally inexhaustible. We become a force of nature, rather than something separated from nature and trying desperately to "make things happen." For instance, with enthusiasm attention is complete. There is no conflict between

focusing on particular things and being aware of the greater environment. At the same time, the energy systems of the body seem purified, especially the cardio-vascular. Indeed, I've noticed that my degree of "physical fitness" alters radically according to the degree and purity of enthusiasm. Inexplicable feats of heroism, like mothers lifting giant trees off their children, or people running for miles in an emergency, are explained by enthusiasm, or complete attention. It's not a miracle, but an extension of perfectly natural capacities. The person who lives their life in enthusiasm is living a heroic life, a life that is a demonstration of human potential. Sport explores this potential, and the feats that can be achieved when it's realized.

Rhythm.

Rhythm is the fundamental aspect of the zone on the physical level. Enthusiasm is synonymous with movement, energy, and when that enthusiasm is pure the Intelligence of nature makes it rhythmic. From within rhythm we can create tempos, beats, and we can also respond with balance to changes in tempo and beat.

Everywhere in the natural world we observe rhythm. We see it in the four seasons, the rising and setting of the sun, the migration of the birds, the hibernation and awakening of the bear, the rhythmic beating of the heart, the inflow and outflow of the breath. Rhythm is the basis of life. Thus, wise athletes and coaches place their emphasis on rhythm. We see this in the way people prepare to play: the tennis player bounces the ball before serving, the batter undergoes the same routine when preparing to receive a pitch, the diver breathes as they stand on the platform. These preparatory affirmations of rhythm create the proper environment for the dynamic activity that follows. In some sports, like tennis, the rhythm and tempo can change with each ball, while, in others, such as long-distance swimming or running, a consistent tempo is the crucial thing, but in every case the sense of rhythm is the very essence of the activity, and pure enthusiasm is the foundation of this beautiful possibility. Thus, when we speak about enthusiasm as a fundamental energy, we aren't lost in a world of abstractions; on the contrary, we're discussing the shortest, most natural path to efficiency and effectiveness.

Try This!

Think and speak in terms of pure enthusiasm and rhythm. To quietly affirm the strength and rhythm of a heartbeat, or the flow of natural breathing, is to dissolve feelings of confusion and trepidation. There is no chaos there, and from within that space we can proceed naturally, purely, happily. Try it and see. Work with athletes to establish natural rhythms in both athletic and non-athletic settings. Sporadic patterns of sleep, for instance, will prove detrimental. Special emphasis should be placed on the natural rhythms before and, where applicable, between athletic exertions. Everything that enhances the feeling of natural rhythm is good, and there are many athletes who would benefit greatly from dance lessons, as also by hearing harmonious music. Think everywhere of rhythm – in eating, sleeping, playing. Pure enthusiasm leads to rhythm, and rhythm leads to everything else.

Concentration.

Enthusiasm is the first key to concentration. True, natural, pure concentration is an effect of enthusiasm. This makes perfect sense, for we pay close attention when we are deeply interested. Your favorite television show is your favorite because you feel a great enthusiasm for it. When you watch that show, do you "try" to concentrate? No, you don't need to try, because the enthusiasm makes the concentration natural and effortless. Thus, if you find that concentration is an effort, or a struggle, you should begin by addressing your enthusiasm for the object of attention.

The greatest liberation.

Legend says that when a potential student asked Sir Lancelot, the great knight of the King Arthur story, how he could become a master swordsman, Lancelot listed three requirements. First, you must train very hard; second, you must be able to focus; and third, you must not care whether you live or die. Upon hearing the last requirement the neophyte's chin dropped, and he walked away.

The pure enthusiast knows the freedom that comes when we are not preoccupied with results. This will sound absurd to many people, but it only shows the huge difference between a qualitative and a quantitative approach to sport and life. The competitor thinks that without his "eye of the tiger" he would sink into laziness. He cannot imagine life without his neuroses. He does not recognize that life itself is striving and the will to blossom. In the natural world we observe great activity, yet there is no "ambition," no notion of "reward," "success," or "failure." So why does anything do anything? What impels the flower to grow, the bird to migrate, the penguin to care for its young? Life - life itself is motion, enthusiasm, and life is very successful, very intelligent, very beautiful. Thus, the enthusiast observes results, he learns from them, he lives and plays with great intensity, great interest, but he is free from fear. If you've ever played in "the zone" then you know exactly what this is like. The freedom from competitiveness is the greatest liberation. This is a grand secret of wisdom, which always directs us to a natural, dynamic life.

🍎 The Enthusiastic Coach 🍎

The first responsibility.

So far we've seen that enthusiasm is crucial for the player. However, it's also the foundation of good coaching. Indeed, the first responsibility of the coach is to recognize, evoke and nurture the enthusiasm of the student.

Try This!

Observe enthusiasm levels. These levels are revealed by the overall atmosphere or "aura" of the player, plus posture, facial expression, speed of movement, etc. I sometimes ask students (usually at the beginning of a lesson) to rate their degree of enthusiasm between zero and ten. If it's less than ten, I ask why, and we don't proceed until the issue is resolved. The resolution may require a discussion, whose aim is to re-kindle inspiration by reminding the student of their love for the game; it may mean canceling a practice, especially if the cause of the depressed energy is fatigue or illness; it may mean doing a favorite drill, one that releases the player into the flow of enthusiasm: If enthusiasm is lacking over a period of time, look to causes, which can range from lack of sleep to fear over results, and see if these can be addressed. Sometimes, a break from the game will be required. This should be considered part of training, since the maintenance of enthusiasm is the precondition of effective training.

The best method.

The best way to encourage and support enthusiasm is to embody and convey it. The enthusiastic coach will radiate a quality that speaks of great energy, and great possibilities. It's true that a coach cannot supply an athlete with enthusiasm, but if the coach feels it in the depths of their being, if it emanates from who they are, then they will inevitably call forth this great energy, wherever it lies latent.

Seriousness and fun the connection?

Pure enthusiasm shouldn't be confused with a "bubbly" personality. Enthusiasm isn't a behavioural tool, a pasted smile, a manipulation. No, true enthusiasm comes straight from the heart, and is totally compatible with focus, or seriousness. Indeed, truly enthusiastic coaches and athletes, who are drawn to their sport like a bee to a flower, find that seriousness, or total interest and absorption, is happiness itself. This ability to combine or unify seriousness and happiness is part of the wisdom of sport. Athletes will get nowhere without discipline and effort, but these musn't be a source of resentment. On the contrary, it is best when they are seen and felt as enjoyable and uplifting. Only pure enthusiasm can produce this beneficial state of affairs. Thus, coaches must equally avoid the pitfalls of aimless "fooling around" and joyless "drilling."

Try This!

Seek for the third option that overcomes both "fooling around" and "drilling." Begin by seeking the proper attitude as you prepare to coach. Before addressing your athletes take a moment to look at and think of them as human beings, as miracles of nature with a vast potential. Can you feel the warmth and broadness of this understanding? Your students will pick it up subconsciously. Feel the responsibility that comes with influencing the growth and development of your fellows, and then proceed. You will demonstrate a synthesis of seriousness and lightness. You are serious about the work of developing human potential and passionate about the medium you have chosen, but you are also good natured. Your students will experience you as one who is more mature than they, detached and dignified and knowing, but also as a warm friend they can trust. This is the natural relation between teacher and student.

Striving versus Stress.

How can we tell if an athlete is being motivated by pure or impure enthusiasm? This is something that coaches and parents will learn as they become immersed in the qualitative approach, and as they apply it to themselves. You will sense the difference, just as you can tell a sweet smell from a sour one. When we smell we distinguish one energy code from another, and it's the same with enthusiasm. Essentially, the person who is moved by pure enthusiasm will be happy, while the one moved by impure enthusiasm will be unhappy. This unhappiness will demonstrate through symptoms of stress. The nervous system of the impure enthusiast is being stimulated along chaotic lines, and this will demonstrate at every level of their being – mental, emotional and physical. Most of us are aware of these symptoms, such as a disinclination to think, extreme emotional reactions, feelings of confusion, the sense that time is going too fast, incessant worry and speculation, feelings of physical heaviness or lack of coordination, muscular tension, headaches, indigestion, and the list goes on. All these things usually indicate that one has placed oneself outside the flow of life; one lacks trust in something greater than one's own brain-ego, so there is insecurity and fear.

The pure enthusiast, on the other hand, is constantly *striving*. They feel a pressure, a dissatisfaction, and this urges them to constantly go on learning, practicing, observing, but their nervous system is being stimulated along natural, rhythmic, harmonious lines, and this feeling of striving and accomplishment, without fear and speculation, is the happiness of the pure enthusiast.

Ending Stress.

When a coach sees symptoms of stress, these should be addressed. We must realize that stress, unhappiness, is neither "natural" nor necessary. This addressing of stress is mainly eliminative – we do not have to learn pure enthusiasm, because it is our natural state – and it can begin at any level. For instance, I once advised a "stressed-out" friend that he have a hot bath and a martini. He did so, and as the tension left his body he was free to engage the mind and understand the causal factors that were the source of the problem. This is a key point: the physical level is never sufficient to eliminate stress. We must engage the mind and activate the heart. With understanding we can eliminate fear and reject the many suggestions of doubt and insecurity which are the true plagues of humanity, and which seem to be running rampant in our present society. A person who demonstrates and shares this understanding is a genuine friend and a true teacher.

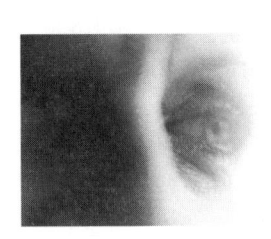

Try This!

Make a list of the symptoms of stress and the features of happiness, as you have experienced and observed them. You might notice that they are often opposites. Record your observations as to what induces stress and what allows enthusiasm to remain pure. Note also what activities, words and thoughts are effective in eliminating stress and affirming happiness. This is simply being responsible for the well-being of oneself and one's students.

🍎 The Power of Enthusiasm 🍎

A simple technique.
The practical power of enthusiasm has led to the development of an extremely effective technique: players, upon entering the athletic venue, or whenever they feel threatened by anxiety or inertia, can consciously affirm their love for the game; they can remind themselves that there's no where in the world they'd rather be. This releases great energy, while dispersing fear.

I remember conveying this advice to a young player, who, upon seeing me a week later, opened his eyes wide, smiled from ear to ear and exclaimed, "Tony, it works!" Indeed, the power of simple enthusiasm is a thrilling thing to discover.

A tapestry of knowledge.
Yes, people will discover many techniques, many ways to affirm and enhance all the great qualities, including enthusiasm. I coach one student who finds that enthusiasm is upgraded when he taps the area around his heart between points This clearly works, for him. We must always remember that the wisdom of sport prescribes a qualitative approach to the game, a foundational and indispensable structure, but not a system that prescribes or imposes set, limited patterns. The intuition and self-knowledge of each person will be the basis for new and effective practices. Out of this great diversity a wonderful tapestry of knowledge will emerge.

Try This!

Study enthusiasm. Specify a certain period of time in which you will observe all things, such as patterns of sleeping, eating and thinking, in terms of their impact on enthusiasm. What releases and maintains a complete, fearless, active absorption in living, and what saps you of this ability? A log book can be maintained in which observations of oneself and others are recorded. Coaches and players can discuss and observe together. This will be very useful. We must become as seriously interested in the great, indispensable qualities as most of us are in other things, like the stock market.

A transforming power.

Recently, while driving a squad of varsity players to an important event, one of the team members, with whom I had been working privately for some time, made an interesting observation. He commented that when it came time for his lessons, all the factors that could've thwarted the success of the session - fatigue, worry, distraction - simply melted away. He said there was something about our lessons that energized him, and always led to the expression of his best tennis. So what was the magic force that had such a transforming effect? Simply this - enthusiasm.

A notable example.

The significance of enthusiasm has been affirmed at the highest levels of sport. For example, in his interview on "Sixty Minutes," no less a player than Andre Agassi explained how his limited success (limited, of course, by his standards), prior to 1994, was due largely to a loss of enthusiasm. His love for the game had been obscured by the hurly-burly of media attention, teen idol-hood, advertising contracts, money, and all the peripheral distractions that come with "fame and fortune." It was only when plagued by injury and facing a personal crisis that he rediscovered that primordial love which releases enthusiasm and leads to greatness. Fame and fortune were subsequently relegated to their proper position as incidental effects, and his ranking soared to number one in the world. What does this tell us?

Is anybody interested?

Yes, the time has come for players, coaches, sport psychologists, researchers and parents to study the scientific value and significance of enthusiasm. By this I don't mean a superficial positiveness, or a certain level of "arousal," but rather a heartfelt, unsullied love of the game, and the people who play it. Enthusiasm is a real, fiery force; it can electrically charge an environment, making it a true hot-bed of creative possibilities. Sincere enthusiasm is the key that unlocks the door, initiating a natural process of never-ending ascent, or improvement. As Helena Roerich says, "the embryo of enthusiasm grows into a beautiful inspiration."

Try This!

Do not underestimate the power and significance of enthusiasm. Enthusiasm isn't just a quaint, childish, adorable feeling, nor is it a fleeting emotion. It's a fundamental energy, and it contains a fabulous intelligence. The ability to recognize and dismiss suggestions and activities, whether mental, verbal or physical, that disturb the purity of enthusiasm requires sincerity and vigilance. It will become a preoccupation for those who see and feel the significance of what is being said.

The first key.

By now, the reader may have guessed that when I discuss enthusiasm I'm speaking from experience, not just propounding a theory. Tennis has been an incredibly strong force in my life. From the time when I was first introduced to the game it has dominated a large proportion of my time and thoughts. My cousin and I, both aged eight, spent four to six hours a day hitting against the backboard at my grandparent's cottage. In this, there was absolutely no "goal." We had no idea where such efforts would lead, and we didn't care. What mattered was the tennis. This purity of approach is the key to fearless, joyous activity of any kind. Indeed, great tennis, as the Zen Masters would say, is egoless, selfless. Athletes confirm this sensation when speaking of "the zone." For the enthusiast, achievements occur within a flow of improvement, a rhythm that is both natural and joyous. Therefore, I say, players, coaches and parents - cultivate enthusiasm, first of all, for it's the fire that lights all other fires, and makes all things possible.

NOBLE TENNIS
THE WISDOM OF SPORT

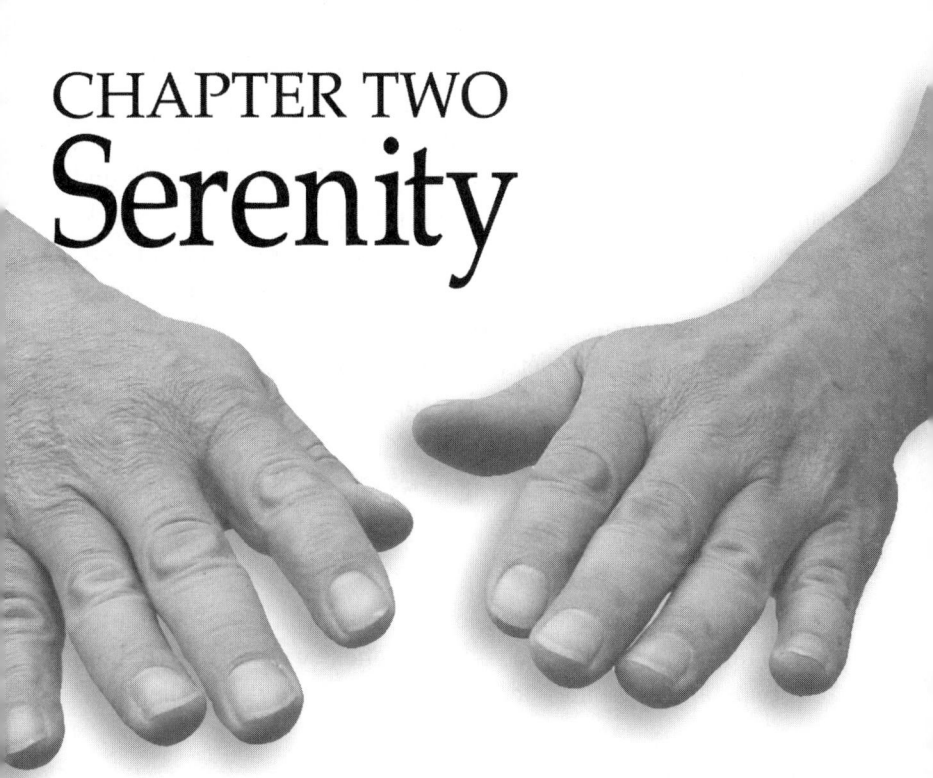

CHAPTER TWO
Serenity

True Power.

When describing the zone, players use words like "peaceful," "calm," "content," "centered." Each of these words describes the action of an identical energy. This energy - serenity - produces true power, where power is understood as the feeling of permanence, stability, immovability, unshakable-ness. This mountain-like serenity involves a complete freedom from irritation, anxiety, anger, frustration, and all fleeting states of mind that lead to dissipation, chaos and unhappiness. Thus, serenity reveals the depths: when we experience true and pure serenity, we feel the very core of our existence; we know ourselves as noble beings whose enormous dignity cannot be touched or swayed by ephemeral, petty things. Serenity is therefore the key to grace and beauty; serenity is happiness; serenity is the zone.

Defining Serenity

The sound of silence.

Serenity is the silence of the lower, egotistical, wanting, fearing self. This taut silence releases our "higher," yet perfectly natural attributes and capacities. Today, this condition is called "the zone."

Try This!

Make silence an integral aspect of life and training. The creation of a calm, fearless atmosphere is the primary responsibility of all. Silence should be introduced as an element of pre and post-match stretching, for instance. Soft music and deep breathing, combined with an emphasis on the rhythmic nature of the movements, will all be helpful in this regard. Trips to parks and gardens may also be useful. The serenity and beauty of nature are powerful ingredients in psychological health. Serenity can be maintained at all times, but familiarity with the feeling must first be attained.

Centripetal force, of course.
Serenity is the feeling that accompanies the action of centripetal energy - that is, energy that moves towards a common center. It's the counterpart of enthusiasm. When the centrifugal and centripetal energies are in perfect harmony, we are in the zone; no, we are the zone.

The center of strength.
The greatest attribute of serenity is quietness, or calmness. All actions are best undertaken from this center of silent strength. It cannot be said enough – serenity is not a lily-livered condition; it has to do with *strength*!

🍎 Serene Enthusiasm 🍎

Buddha's racquet.
It is said that the Buddha had a major awakening, or moment of increased understanding, when he overheard a teacher instructing his pupil on how to string a musical instrument (which could easily have been a tennis or squash racquet!). The teacher said, "if the strings are too loose, they won't play, and if they're too tight, they snap." Hearing this, the Buddha realized that all constructive energies and attributes must be harmonized. Anyone who experiments with enthusiasm and serenity will realize that he was right.

The vigor of serenity.
The harmonization of enthusiasm and serenity has not been achieved by those who are often called "laid back." Usually, these people are just lazy. In the zone, serenity is characterized by a great intensity, because it's conjoined with enthusiasm and guided by a sense of purpose. The serenity of the mountain is a formidable serenity, not a limpid one! Thus, serenity is not opposed to vigorous activity. The serene individual, being free from fear and irritation, and from an impatient desire for immediate results, discovers that their mind is free to concentrate, fully, upon whatever is being done. This undivided attention releases enormous amounts of energy and opens the gate to the power of rhythm, thereby producing efficiency and effectiveness. Thus, serenity, far from opposing action, or enthusiasm, is precisely what allows it to be unbroken, balanced and joyful.

The synthesis of the zone.
Without pure enthusiasm, joyous progress is inconceivable, and serenity is just a synonym for inertia - a "stress buster" promoted by self-help gurus and designed to relieve us from the impure enthusiasm that's inspired by fear. This is how serenity comes to be falsely associated with inertia, with a "lotus-land" of inactivity. However, without serenity, enthusiasm is a more-or-less blind and undirected force, as is seen, for instance, in those at the adolescent stage of human development. Here there is movement, both physical and psychological, but no rhythm. Grace-in-action and right living, or maturity, come when enthusiasm and serenity are united. Thus, the athlete who is in the zone will be *serenely enthusiastic*.

Simplicity.
People will ask, how can I attain serenity? How can I feel the

NOBLE ⊙ TENNIS
THE WISDOM OF SPORT

strength and calmness of inner stability and rhythm? But perhaps it would be better to ask – how can you not feel this way? Why would you not? Athletes lose serenity because they lose simplicity. They are not simply playing. Instead, they are speculating, wondering who is watching, etc. They are doing everything but playing! Sport is no longer simply sport; it is a dramatic opera, a great drama with heroes and villains, success and failure, fame and fortune, health and social standing. In this way, the sport, the actual activity, and all its power to instill qualities and produce beauty, is lost in a hub-bub whose content is mainly imaginary, speculative. Our *interest* in playing is lost, or, at the very least, divided amongst other interests, and so there is fragmentation, confusion, stress. This can all be ended in one single moment, one instant of stillness, one affirmation of inward strength and rhythm, one feeling of innocent involvement in the real, the actual, the now. In short, if we shut-up for two seconds and simply engage the game, there is serenity.

Try This!

One of the best ways to recover a lost sense of serenity is to simply listen to the natural rhythm of your heartbeat, or the inflow and outflow of breath. This returns us to natural simplicity and rhythm. However, as understanding is increased, a single thought will often prove sufficient. Thus, the more juvenile ideas and preoccupations can be dismissed as we say, "I am simply here to play." In this way, the self-created opera will be seen as silly, and the whole structure will dissolve before the power of an understanding smile. Eventually, not even words will be required, as our whole feeling about what we are doing and why can be re-oriented in silence. Silence and feeling are powerful.

The Elevated Attitude.

Enthusiasm remains pure and serenity is stabilized as the athlete begins to feel that fear and doubt are *beneath* them. It's like the Knights of the Round Table in the story of King Arthur. Their focus was on honor and dignity, and the arts they learned, such as horsemanship and swordsmanship, were expressions of these attributes and ideals, these great possibilities. When sport is viewed from such a height, it is imbued with quality, nobility, and serenity blossoms as the expression of an inner strength that cannot be touched by that which is ignoble. Anger and distraction are sensed as belittling, they are dismissed as options, and hence they die a natural death. In this way, the athlete stands on a plateau that is above and beyond the chaotic realm of distractions and egocentric ambitions that produce corruption and decay. This elevation of attitude is the key to serenity, and I have found that athletes will respond very positively to the suggestion that they are pure, *free* from the puny world of strictly selfish ambition. True, reason can show that speculation, fear and doubt are unnecessary, and experience will prove them to be ineffective, but nothing so effectively *eliminates* them from the human psyche as the feeling that they are contemptible.

The Problem of Analysis

A hindrance revealed.

I'd like to discuss the phrase "paralysis of analysis." It indicates that analysis disrupts serenity. Hence, the constant babbling of the analytic mind is a hindrance to nobility and greatness. Coaches and players who focus exclusively on technical, strategic, or even mental minutia create great obstacles for themselves.

Control mania!

The analytic mind craves control. It tries to hold things still so it can dissect them, but all sports are living, moving activities. Sport proceeds along holistic, intuitive, rhythmic lines. Hence, the essence of greatness is artistic inspiration, not "critical thinking," and inspiration comes with serenity.

The analytic scramble.

The speculations of the analytic mind are spurred on by fear. For instance, players often panic when they make errors. They instantly lose serenity, and then scramble to correct this mistake or that. However, their ability to analyze and control can't keep pace with the speed of actual events, and the result is great frustration. Even when the analysis is theoretically perfect, the absence of serenity and the constantly shifting circumstances make it futile. What a dilemma!

Try This!

Constantly recommend serenity over analytic thought. If, during a match, nervousness begins to set in, begin by taking a few deep breaths. When the feeling of quiet has been restored, proceed. Practice this, perhaps with the aid of key phrases. With one student I recommended that he say, " I observe, I do not react." After serenity has been restored, observations and refinements can be made, but this will look and feel very different from the analytic control mania.

Observation to the rescue.

When seeking a solution to the problem of analysis, many people decide "it's best not to think." But thought is absolutely necessary in learning. Besides, thought is natural, so the suppression of thought is an act of violence, and violence is no partner of serenity. The real solution is to recognize that analysis is only one form of thought. We can leave the maze of analysis behind, and replace it with observation. The serene mind will calmly observe. It will realize that while technical adjustments may be necessary, they must take place within the sphere of joyous serenity. The trick, therefore, is not to stop thinking, but to think calmly. This may seem like a trifling distinction to some, but it's extremely significant. Analysis is laced with fear; observation is free.

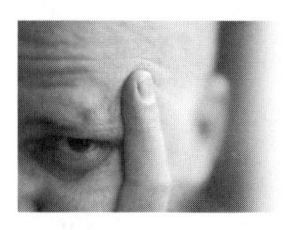

Try This!

Remember that serenity is fully compatible with close observation. Test yourself or your students on their observational skills. See who notices little changes in the environment. Serenity creates an attentiveness that is totally free of fear and judgment. Analytic babble, like all forms of speculation, separates us from reality. Serenity, on the other hand, connects us with what is actually *going on, and this has major implications in terms of rhythm and coordination. Serenity is like being in the flow of a river. The desire to get outside the river and control the flow is the big problem.*

The flow of events.

Observation is effective because it proceeds *without judgment*. The serene individual observes the flow of events. They do not label things as "good" or "bad," and then proceed to think. Emotional elation and frustrated irritation are equally opposed to serenity, and there can be no constructive thought without serenity.

The open mind.

Judgments of good and bad are based on preconceived notions, ideas, or images. We have a static notion of an outcome, such as "winning," and we judge everything against it. This makes us reactionaries. Learning stops. With serenity, on the other hand, the mind is *open*, and we are constantly learning and applying. With serenity, there is no failure.

Try This!

Practice non-judgment. Have practice sessions whose only theme is the complete absence of evaluation in terms of good and bad, right and wrong. Similarly, ask athletes to relate what they have observed during a match or a drill, or indeed in any context, and clarify when what they are offering is a judgment. For instance, if you ask for observations on a match and you hear "I played like crap," realize that's an evaluation, not an observation. In serenity, we observe and refine, we learn, and this is a totally different feeling from that of judging.

Serenity In Action

Confidence defined.

Serenity gives content to the vague notion of confidence. Confidence is not "a positive self-image." As long as there is the need to project an image of oneself, there is precisely a *lack* of confidence. In serenity, we don't doubt who or what we are, so we don't set up a conflict between here and there, now and later, what we are and what we hope to become. Confidence indicates the ability to live here and now. It is the companion of serenity.

Try This!

Recognize that serenity cannot be forced into existence. It comes when the lower nature, the site of fear and mental babbling, is quiet. Thus, our primary work is to address and eliminate the ideas and preoccupations that produce fear and analysis. This is an ongoing project, requiring observation and communication over time. I recommend discussions and activities whose theme is serenity, but, best of all, I recommend developing the alertness that notices opportunities as they arise. This alertness is born when the significance of serenity is recognized.

The Tony Turn-Around.

A few years back I was playing Varsity tennis for Queen's University in Kingston, Ontario, Canada. In one memorable match I was behind 4-1 in the first set, and was not playing my best. Then, having switched ends, I spontaneously walked up very close to the back tarp (the heavy fabric that separates one set of courts from another), so that my back was turned to my opponent, closed my eyes for a few seconds and said to myself, "that's enough." I then turned around, and I was a completely different person. My posture was upright, my movements were rhythmic and strong, my focus was undivided, my shots lacked any hesitation. I won the set and the match, 6-4, 6-2.

This action of going close to the tarp and then emerging in a transformed state was later named "the Tony turn-around." My team-mates inquired as to what I actually did in these moments, and I found it difficult to respond. Now I realize that I was initiating a process through which enthusiasm was purified and serenity realized. When I said, "that's enough" I obliterated every distraction, every non-essential factor from mind and body. This was preceded by the creation of a space that was isolated from the atmosphere which had bred these impure ingredients – hence the closeness to the tarp and the closed eyes. I was alone for a moment, returning to myself after having been lost in a web of worldly distractions, and from within that stability I could re-emerge, being "in the world, but not of it," so to speak, and all the rest followed.

Try This!

In the story of the "Tony turn-around" we see the essential outlines of a process that is universally applicable. First, there is silence, whose importance cannot be over-stated. This is aided by a temporary feeling of detachment from the outward environment. Hence we see athletes putting towels over their heads, or just bowing their head downwards and looking at their shoelaces, or their racquet strings. We see similar rhythms of momentary abstraction in the regular routines of baseball pitchers, for instance, and many other examples could be furnished. It is the crucial process of isolating oneself from the worldly, with all its distractions and psychological snares, and uniting with an inward realm of serenity and strength. Thus, the position of the athlete could be called one of "isolated unity." From within the detached silence, there is no chaos, no noise, no clutter. All the rest follows. My "turn around" included some words, and these embodied a thought that affirmed serenity. Such words may or may not be necessary. They normally won't be when the process is proceeding naturally – when the player is in the zone, but a supportive phrase will often prove useful when the athlete is struggling to regain a position of serenity. In all this there is no need for distinctly Pavlovian methods. The essential understanding and requirements need to be clarified and discussed and experienced, but it is best when the particulars are left to the spontaneous intelligence of the athlete. This makes of serenity something that is familiar and intimate and valuable. People can never feel this way when they are imposing a theory that comes from the outside.

A new buzz word.

In the world of physical training and physical prowess, one hears a great deal about such things as strength, speed, endurance and agility. But there is one word that is rarely mentioned, and that is *suppleness*. True, we do speak about flexibility, but few actually stress this component, and even fewer understand the practical significance of the term. It is seen merely as a way to avoid injury, and is not connected with rhythm and grace. This narrow view is insufficient, and stems partly from our failure to comprehend the nature and significance of serenity.

NOBLE ● TENNIS
THE WISDOM OF SPORT

The great athletes always demonstrate superior responsiveness. Their competence is largely an effect of the complete absence of tension, or unnecessary flexing of the muscles. This is a physical effect of serenity. Under these conditions, there is no inhibition, no artificial limitation, no resistance through which they have to play, and this means that rhythm and mobility are unimpeded. Indeed, strength without suppleness is of very limited value.

Thus, I suggest a new buzz word: suppleness.

Try This!

During on-court sessions, address serenity as an aspect of efficiency and effectiveness. Is what you observe a technical or physical inability, or is it the result of tension? How can you know if it's a genuine technical problem when the cause may be purely inward? Would this still be a problem if there were suppleness and rhythm, which come with enthusiasm and serenity? Thus, when I stop a drill, it is often to ask, "who is playing here?" Is this enthusiasm and serenity in a process of learning, in which case we have a technical area to address, or not? Do not assume that your technical chatter is going to be useful when mental babbling and emotional turmoil are precisely the problems at hand. Also, observe bodily tension. A lack of tension in the mouth and jaws, combined with an almost "droopy" feeling around the eyes, are sure signs of serenity. Sometimes the simple action of relaxing a clenched jaw or letting the shoulders fall will be valuable as a first step on the road to calmness. Self-conscious tension must be addressed in all learning environments. *The absence of calmness cuts off all your natural rhythm and coordination, your instinctive intelligence, and makes learning almost impossible.*

Acceptance.

Recently, I've made major advances in the realm of serenity. For some time I've known that I'm a good tennis player. However, the depth of that knowledge was limited. I still had doubts. This showed itself in a distinctive way: when I played well I became very excited. This indicated a degree of surprise on my part, a kind of childish excitement, and this contributed to the loss of many matches where I had the early lead. My elation caused me to rush, I became fatigued, my mind zipped into future discussions and future matches, and this was very detrimental to how I was playing in the here and now. As the tide turned, I became confused; serenity was squandered. I berated myself for thinking into the future along what seemed like egotistical lines, and for my lack of discipline, but I finally recognized that serenity was the real issue in all this, and I have now learned to *accept* that I can play at a high level. Thus, serenity is unshaken, even by success.

A guidance system.

The achievement of serenity, which is the silence of the lower, opens us to a higher guidance or intuition. When to be utterly silent and absorbed? When to make a technical change? What to do between points? Fear not. You'll know what to do, and no behavioural psychology is required. Until we accept that there is a natural form of intelligence that is greater than our little, separate, speculating, analyzing mind, the zone, with all its happiness, rhythm and effectiveness, will remain a closed book, a mystery.

The drooling idiot.

Meditation and breathing exercises are designed to make us familiar with the composed or integrated state of being that is serenity. There's nothing glamorous about this condition, or these practices. Indeed, there's a great coach who advises that the player who is in the zone will look like "a drooling idiot." If you doubt this, just look at the facial expression of the great tennis players as they prepare to return serve, or basketball players before a free throw - the mouth hangs open, the eyes don't blink, the skin is totally relaxed; they're like focused zombies! The zone is a condition in which higher, purer, more refined energies act in and through us, but for this to happen, the "lower self" must be utterly quiescent – "dumb," but ultimately receptive.

Try This!

Employ serenity exercises, like deep breathing, as introductory aids. Even five minutes per day will be useful. All that really matters is the sense of familiarity with the feeling of serenity. The form of these exercises is not particularly important. You can count your breaths, up to ten and then start over, or just breath and be quiet, or just look attentively and appreciatively out a window! Make sure the posture is correct while doing any such work. I did this with one student who noted that the first few times five minutes felt like five hours, but it got easier and easier each day. Indeed, most people are sadly unfamiliar with the feeling of disciplined stillness. Ultimately, meditation can be undertaken on a busy street corner, and why not, for it is simply an attentive frame of mind.

A special wisdom.

Serenity is a special wisdom. It transcends conventional ways of thinking and acting. Enthusiasm is the source of all motion – it is molten lava, but serenity is the agent that harmonizes all things. Since the keynote of sport is harmony, serenity must be the foundation of athletic greatness.

NOBLE TENNIS
THE WISDOM OF SPORT

CHAPTER THREE
Patience

Patience

Patience is a virtue,
That is what they say,
So let us take a closer look,
Delve into this cliché.

Enthusiasm keeps us moving,
Ever on the go,
But patience stands and kneads the bread,
Rhythmic, steady, slow.

The patient mind will comprehend
The way things really work:

The tree will grow and then it dies,
It crumbles in the sand,
But give it time and you will hold
A diamond in your hand!

NOBLE TENNIS
THE WISDOM OF SPORT

🍎 Understanding Patience 🍎

Serenity in action.
Patience and serenity are inseparable. Serenity is a composed state of being, and patience is serenity in action.

Wait!
In the simplest terms, patience indicates the willingness to wait. This is crucial, because it reveals that patience concerns what is *not* done, what is omitted. For instance, any preconceived notion, any prejudice, any idea of a specific outcome runs counter to serenity, and hence to patience. Thus, the noble athlete is silent or inactive in relation to these activities. This silence is patience – the willingness to put one foot after another, without frenetic worrying, speculating and fearing. The noble athlete plays, observes, learns, and plays some more. As for results, they follow the best advice, which is – wait and see.

The peril of irritation.
The purpose of patience is not to suppress irritation. Where there is irritation, the situation should be addressed and resolved, not doggedly and stubbornly borne in the name of some ambition or goal. When irritation threatens, the first thing we must do is "stop!" Irritation, like a wave on the ocean, becomes bigger as it gains momentum. This momentum is quelled by a moment of silence, stillness, inaction – or, in other words, applied serenity, patience. Thus, the best procedure is to notice the irritation, and then get quiet – perhaps close your eyes, take a few deep breaths, look at a nearby tree or flower, feel the breeze in your face, listen to the birds, relax the jaw, unsquint the eyes. In this atmosphere, you can proceed constructively.

Thought as an ally.

Proceeding in patience may or may not require thought. Persistent or recurring irritation may lead to questions, and these will lead to the understanding that obliterates obstacles. Why are you irritated? Is it perhaps that your expectations, of yourself or of another, have been disappointed? Why do you have such expectations, such images, such fantasies? Are they productive, or do they breed fear and distraction? These are the real issues. Patience allows us to address and dissolve these issues, so, obviously, to define patience as the avoidance or suppression of crucial opportunities for growth is totally inappropriate.

Dissolving irritation.

Once, when I was coaching the Queen's Varsity team, our number one player was struggling. At the changeovers we had been discussing various aspects of the match, but nothing seemed to work. He was becoming irritated Then, when he was trailing 5-2 in the second set, having already lost the first, he sat down in his chair, bent his head forward, closed his eyes, and became very quiet. Later, he told me he was simply listening to the sound of his heart beating. I did not interfere with this quiet but poignant exercise. From that moment forward, he was brilliant. He won the match, and all because he followed the correct procedure when faced with irritation, and its accompanying lack of rhythm, coordination and joy.

Try This!

Develop the ability to notice irritation when it begins. Insensitivity allows little problems to develop into big problems. Irritation, unaddressed, overwhelms its victims. Thus, when practicing, do not let irritation flourish. Follow a three step procedure: 1) notice, 2) stop, get quiet, and 3) proceed, observe, learn, enjoy.

Patience and enthusiasm.

Perseverance is another important element of patience. It connects patience with enthusiasm. Serenity and enthusiasm work together. Enthusiasm moves us forward, pushing us past all obstacles, past all contentment with past achievements, past all rest or inactivity. Serenity, on the other hand, collects, gathers, composes; it tends towards completion and wholeness. When we can participate in the constant striving of enthusiasm without losing a basic sense of serenity, we are the zone, and patience is ever-present in the zone. Patience is the act of striving constantly forward, but without desperation, without grasping, without greediness, fear and worry. Thus, again, patience is *inaction*, a great "doing nothing" when it comes to speculation and the childish desire for instant completion, and patience is *action* when it comes to sustained striving and learning.

Try This!

Realize that patience must be connected and united with enthusiasm and serenity. Patience without enthusiasm is ugly; it's a kind of suffering. And patience without serenity isn't patience at all, but the suppression of a time bomb. Patience as stubbornness and resentment must be removed. We replace these with patience as the great joy of constant learning, free from fear. Only when patience is based in enthusiasm and serenity can we affirm the old cliché which says that "patience is a virtue." The wise coach will stress patience because it alone ensures that lack of familiarity with sustained effort will not dampen enthusiasm or transform serenity into its opposite, its nemesis - irritation.

Patience in the flow.

With patience, we can take delight in a process, appreciating all the steps along the way, without interfering or forcing. This requires trust, a broad perspective, an open mind, respect for others, a sense of humor and, above all, fearlessness. Patience is a great achievement; it is the hallmark of the mature mind.

🍎 Patience and the Student 🍎

Student-ness.

It's widely recognized that coaches must demonstrate patience, but patience is also the key to being a good student. The responsibility of students for their student-ness is something we all-too-often overlook, or forget. The purpose of coaching is to teach, but you can't teach without students, and being a student means demonstrating a capacity for *sustained* listening and practicing. Thus, patience is the foundation of student-hood. If patience is lacking, then true coaching - which is a serenely enthusiastic exchange, a flow of labor and communication that isn't hampered by impatience and moods - will never take place, and a patch-work of technical programming and "behaviour modification" is all that will remain.

The Dramatist.

There is a type of person who loves drama, and many athletes fall into this category. For them, as Shakespeare said, all the world

NOBLE TENNIS
THE WISDOM OF SPORT

is but a stage, and we are merely players! Such a person can never really embrace patience, which exalts simplicity and constancy. They demand constant changes in plot, setting and mood. The drama of the moment is what matters, and they revel in the glare of the spotlight, the act of being on stage. This person thrives in controversy. In their play, they are the protagonist - the striving, struggling hero or victim, and they are surrounded by enemies. The star of the play rants and fights against the elements, against injustice, failure, defeat, a cruel fate. To them, patience would seem like the borification of life. Patience deals in reality, takes delight in reality. It is not glamorous, but solid and joyous. The patient individual will change as they learn, but the dramatist never really learns anything, and therefore never really changes; they just play parts, and sometimes they play them very well. Jimmy Connors, for instance, is a dramatist. When he steps on to the court, he shouts out to the world – "it's show-time!"

The wise coach will recognize this type. He or she will neither fret nor try to change them, but will recognize them for what they are. They will look on with humor, while making sure that the dramatist does not try to get others to play unsavory roles for the sake of their play! The hero needs fervent supporters, filled with emotion and anxiety, hanging on the fate of the hero, and vile enemies, whose darkness serves to highlight the glorious brilliance of the hero. The wise coach is not particularly interested in these roles. They are not interested in the constant attempts of the dramatist to get everyone focused on and involved in their play, as though it were the most crucial thing in the universe. The coach will walk off the set. Or, respecting the character of the person, and matching them tit-for-tat, they may perhaps convince the actor that the time has come for them to play their best and most challenging role - the role of the infinitely patient person! After all, the best actors are those who get totally lost in their role, and, for the athlete, this means getting totally involved in the mastery of the game. When this occurs, sport becomes a demonstration of noble qualities, as opposed to a mere show of smoke and mirrors.

Developing patience.

How to develop patience? There are countless ways. You can implement volume training that extends attentional endurance: do an exercise whose completion requires three hundred repetitions (or, conversely, one that requires a small number of precise, difficult actions, properly executed); play practice matches whose sole criteria for success is perfect composure; have students execute an athletic action in slow motion, seeing who can be the most detailed (this is excellent for physical or kinesthetic awareness, as well as patience); teach kids to sit quietly, to pay complete attention when others are speaking, and to cut out restless fidgeting; engage in discussions where groups of athletes consider various matters, such as strategy or current affairs, in a sustained way, or where they have to bring themselves to bear on a puzzle, a mystery, or a brain-teaser; encourage reading; always address anger and impatience - get to their causes, which are usually fear-related, and root them out; and, above all, cultivate enthusiasm and serenity at all times.

Try This!

When doing drills or activities whose theme is patience, be sure to match the duration of the exercise to the experience of the student. Do drills that will definitely take them beyond their usual degree of patience, but do not carry the exercise to extremes that will harm the quality of the work, or lead to injury. We must be patient, even as we strive for patience, lest we end up like the person who says, "Lord, grant me patience, and grant it to me right now!"

A good example.

In the film "The Karate Kid" there's a great demonstration of how a coach instills patience. The lead character, the student, is instructed to paint a giant fence, using a very specific technique. This he does, with great care and perseverance, only to be told that he must now apply a second coat! Finally, after several similar exercises, the student rebels against what seems like irrelevant labor, only to discover that each of his chores represent perfect moves and postures in karate, which have now become instinctive. This is wise coaching: the quality, patience (and, in this case, trust and discipline as well), receives emphasis, and the technique is considered an effect, or corollary, of this qualitative achievement.

The wisdom of patience.

The value of patience, as the foundational requirement for all training and relationship, is understood in the East to a far greater extent than in the West. In China, for instance, there's a great master of tai chi. Those who wish to become his pupils must fulfill a simple requirement - they must come to the park where he works, each day at sunrise, and practice. If they do this for three years, then they are eligible, but not guaranteed, to join his group. Just imagine the readiness, the enthusiasm and patience, of the student who undertakes this program and succeeds! Thus, by insisting on this regimen, the teacher is already teaching. He is transforming enthusiasts into students, while eliminating those who are merely curious, or momentarily intrigued. He is a wise and patient coach.

Try This!

When taking on new students, assess patience levels and, where necessary, do drills or assign work that will test and enhance this quality. This may require a stated "preliminary" period, in which you learn whether or not the player is capable of being a student. It is perfectly acceptable to inform students of the purpose underlying this preliminary work.

🍎 Patience-in-Action 🍎

The psychological immune system.

The beneficial influence of patience is obvious, and this applies whether we observe from a psychological, tactical, or physical-technical point of view. For instance, the patient person, by definition, is immune to almost every form of psychological disturbance. Anger, irritation and frustration- the "big three" for athletes - are all synonyms for impatience. They represent an inability for sustained striving and waiting. Wise coaches realize that these destructive forces are ruinous for the player, not to mention the person, but they are often ignorant as to the true causes of these maladies. They then resort to behavioural psychology and extrinsic or materialistic motivations, but these aren't serious solutions; they treat the symptoms, but not the disease. So why resort to patch-work psychology when the obliteration of obstacles is a possibility? Cultivate serenity and patience, and the destructive impulses will lack the fertile soil in which to germinate.

One thing, or ten million?

Tactically, it can be observed that a large proportion of strategical errors result from rash and premature - i.e. impatient - actions. Thus, before we outline the ten million scenarios of any given sport, we should first cultivate that quality which, in and of itself, instills a serene ability to wait, to observe, and to treat a point, or a match, or a life, as a process, building it as an architect designs a house - intuitively, intelligently, cooperatively and patiently. Again, we must recognize that to demand behaviours, while failing to cultivate the psychological attributes that make them natural and necessary, is hypocritical; it misses the entire point of training and playing, which is the blossoming forth of people, not just players.

Patient technique.

In tennis, the serve is perhaps the greatest example of a shot that requires patience. Prior to the actual serve there is "the ritual": that process through which the server collects their energies and comes to a point of tension or silence. This is a moment of poignant waiting. Often, at this point, the facial expression will be totally blank: the energy of serenity is permeating the entire self, and patience is being instilled and expressed.

Then there's the motion. Here, again, patience predominates. As the body moves, the server appears to be acting in slow motion. A rhythmic movement leads to that moment of nearly suspended animation when the racquet is poised in the "back-scratch" position and the ball seems to be hovering in space. At this point, explosive enthusiasm asserts itself, and the collected energy is released - upward, outward and forward. Even now, however, patience is expressed - the motion is not jerky, but continuous, graceful and disciplined; there is no premature grasping, no rushing to get it over with.

It's true that these matters can be discussed in purely technical terms. We can talk about premature weight transfer, the tossing motion, etc., but the point is that many of these detrimental behaviours are merely *effects* of impatience. So why not deal with them at a causal level? In many cases, it's good if a coach can correct technical errors without even mentioning them. Technical discussions are dangerous – they lead the unwary traveler into the realm of analysis - and we should approach with caution.

Try This!

Get used to using the language of the qualitative approach. Discuss tactical and technical elements in terms of patience. Let students experiment. Ask them to hit their usual serve, but to apply patience from start to finish. See what happens.

NOBLE 🎾 TENNIS
THE WISDOM OF SPORT

🍎 Patience and Society 🍎

Patience: a virtue?

Modern society wages an incessant war against patience. Instant gratification is the modern motto, and the ideal consumer is necessarily repulsed by the idea of waiting. Indeed, full-blooded consumerism requires a grasping compulsiveness. Hence, the consumer (as we are now called, instead of human beings) is meant to be eternally dissatisfied - frustrated with their inability to attain and possess all things, now. We are meant to be examples of impure or selfish enthusiasm, with no serenity to balance and measure the movement. Processes, in this case, are just irritating by-paths. Indeed, the only reason we accept the process is because it seems unavoidable, and, if a short-cut should present itself, we take it without hesitation. This, of course, is the principle of all economic scams, not to mention steroid use, etc. We all become indignant when we hear of these things, but this is slightly hypocritical. How can we bemoan what is only the logical outcome, the natural extension, of the causes we are ourselves initiate and support? These "criminals" have merely perfected the qualities that most of us demonstrate in a partial, luke-warm way. When we have *eliminated* these things, then mere bitching will stop, and the presentation of actual solutions will begin.

The victory of impatience.

The modern shortage of patience finds expression in athletic venues all over the world. Even in the past ten years one observes a clear deterioration of this noble quality. Once, the neurotic behaviour of young John Mcenroe was the exception. Today, it can be seen at virtually any provincial or national event, and also at the club level.

The re-instatement of patience is a great and important task. It involves the celebration of learning and a sense of the inherent dignity of each person. The noble athlete recognizes irritation as an immature, irresponsible, overly theatrical response to what is actually a challenge and an opportunity.

CHAPTER FOUR
Concentration

Foundations of concentration.

Concentration, like patience, is best understood as a companion of enthusiasm and serenity. True, we can force ourselves to "pay attention!" by a violent act of the personal will, but the concentration of the zone is always linked with a pervasive calmness and ease. Hence, just as enthusiasm needs to become serene enthusiasm, concentration requires a foundation of calm strength. When concentration is united with serenity and pure enthusiasm, its character is fundamentally altered, and what was once a painful discipline becomes a natural, revealing, joyous state of being.

A sensible request.

Unnan says, "if you walk, just walk; if you sit, just sit. But whatever you do, don't wobble!" That's a statement about concentration. Concentration eliminates half-way-ness, and that is the simple secret of its effectiveness.

Concentration Defined

A practical synthesis.

Concentration has been practically defined as "an intoxicating involvement in what is happening, and the freedom to watch it happen." In other words, Concentration is the practical synthesis of enthusiasm and serenity. Pure, innocent enthusiasm is precisely "an intoxicating involvement in what is happening," and serenity always leads to that detachment and dispassion, that patience and attentiveness, which provide "the freedom to watch it happen." Thus, when we combine enthusiasm and serenity, we have concentration, and, conversely, when we concentrate, we enhance or fortify enthusiasm and serenity.

The open mind.
Concentration can be understood very simply as *unbiased watching, or looking*. This sounds easy, but most people never look at something without a preconceived notion or image, a pre-set desire or ambition, a personal prejudice that's built right into the looking. Most people, in other words, have a closed and conditioned mind. When we approach a thing, like a tennis ball, or allow it to approach us, with a completely silent, focused, attentive mind, we are concentrating, and this concentration is a powerful, informative, beautiful thing. Concentration allows us to respond spontaneously and freely in a dynamic, athletic setting, and this freedom and spontaneity is the joy of the zone. In concentration, or true open-mindedness, dynamic harmonization becomes a natural disposition, and the mind and body fulfill their creative functions.

Misunderstandings.
When people are in a truly concentrated state, the muscles of the body are very relaxed. Often, the facial expression is completely blank. Clearly, then, it's a mistake to associate concentration with the furling of the brow, the gritting of the teeth, the straining of the eyes and the tensing of the muscles. And yet concentration is commonly understood in precisely these terms. It's seen as a Herculean effort to "block everything out," thereby *limiting* our sphere of attention; it is seen, in short, as a form of resistance, and as something we forcefully *impose* upon ourselves, in a desperate attempt to repel the fears and distractions that normally plague the mind. This willful concentration is hard work, but is it necessary? The answer is this: such rigorous and painful techniques are only required when serenity is lacking; for, if there is no fear and no doubt, what's there to resist? Thus, we don't need fear as a motivator. Beauty can also motivate, and, when it

does, concentration becomes inclusive, not exclusive; joyous, not grim; serene, not uptight.

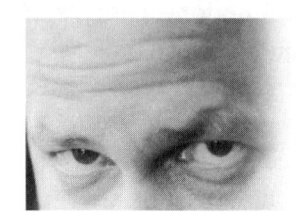

Try This!

Have discussions where the true nature of concentration is considered. Concentration is so confused with violence and personal will that some clarification is badly needed.

Why Does it Work?

The human sponge.

Every athletic scenario is filled with information. When we concentrate, when we watch with total attention, we absorb that information like a sponge, and we learn to respond in harmony with the requirements of the scenario. Then, because we have responded, we will increasingly find ourselves in the right place, and creative action will be possible. Thus, reception is about harmony, and projection is about creativity. Concentration makes them both possible. But all this needs to be tried out, tested. Yes, you must *see* for yourself!

In the spotlight.

Concentration eliminates fear and doubt, and these are the primary sources of all under-achievement. Fear and doubt are based on speculation; their keynote is "what if?" - what if I lose, what if I look like an idiot, what if my ranking drops, etc. etc. When we concentrate, when we are "in the now," such considerations cease to exist. This freedom from negative and egotistical speculation is a great liberation. It leads to a fuller participation in life. The

NOBLE 🎾 TENNIS
THE WISDOM OF SPORT

mind, which is normally scattered and fragmentary, becomes like a focused spotlight, bringing its fullness to bear on each moment. This, in turn, increases our ability to observe, respond and act. Thus, concentration releases potential by encouraging serenity, and freeing enthusiasm from the bondage of fear. The achievement and stabilization of concentration constitutes a central aim of athletic training.

Try This!

Demonstrate the energy of concentration to yourself and your students. I have walked before whole groups of people and changed the entire atmosphere by becoming quiet, focused and powerful in their midst. They see and feel the collection of energy, the deep focused silence, the penetrating look, the deep joy and interest, the love of life and potential. This works well at the beginning of a lesson, or when groups of kids are getting too hyper, or if a team is nervous. Concentration is a transforming energy, and it creates a dynamic environment.

The OJ connection.

Concentration can be understood in terms of natural science. It occurs in the same way that orange juice becomes concentrated orange juice - namely, by the removal of all that is non-essential to the orange-ness of the orange. When the water is gone, the concentrated juice, the essence of the orange, remains. Similarly, when people remove from themselves all traces of fear, distraction and doubt, a concentrated state remains. The result is an ability to bring oneself entirely, completely, singly into whatever one is doing. This, in turn, releases great energy, leading to enhanced efficiency, attentiveness and adaptability; or, in other words, to the creative zone. Thus, concentration is a focused or purified state of being, achieved mainly by the *elimination* of thoughts and feelings that lead to a scattering of forces.

Try This!

Never use fear or threats as spurs to concentration, and do not appeal to selfish ambition. These are the very energies that stifle the greater potential and happiness of the human being. The release of that potential is the fundamental concern, and it alone can provide sufficient motivation and reward. Therefore, stress what is humanly good and humanly possible, and the peculiar way that each will express these things. Make that the goal, and strive relentlessly in that direction. This is not a trifling distinction; it's a different space from which to work.

🎾 Working With Concentration 🎾

Using both eyes.

When I was attending the All-Canadian tennis academy, I received an extremely significant lesson from the resident squash pro, Mac Kerim, a former world champion. He was an elderly, Egyptian man, with silvery hair and deep, gray eyes. Occasionally Mac taught tennis, and when I arrived early one day he offered to feed me a few balls. After watching me hit several mediocre groundstrokes, Mac called me to the net. He said, "watch the ball."

I replied, rather obstinately, "I am watching the ball."

He said, "no, you watch the ball with one eye; watch it with two - watch it with both eyes."

This simple advice had a transforming effect. Mac was absolutely correct - I wasn't really, totally watching the ball. When I followed his instructions and focused my attention, it was like entering a different world: the ball appeared bigger, and it seemed to be moving slower then before - I had time to prepare; I felt a great inflow of psychic and physical energy; self-conscious nervousness and worry could not occur; irritation and distraction were impossible; joy was present. Mac had offered a lesson in concentration, and that would become the theme of my tennis for the next three years.

Try This!

Where concentration is deficient, deal with causes. Is it a lack of familiarity with sustained attention? Then work progressively in this area, through on and off-court exercises. Is it that fear and doubt are constantly causing the mind to wander? Then address fear. Is it a lack of enthusiasm? Then address that. The ability to recognize the source of any lack will grow through communication and experience.

Wait and see revisited.

I refer you once again to the simple phrase, "wait and see." This is a formula for the enlightened handling of many situations, and it's not as passive as it may seem. Waiting and seeing are both actions. Again, if irritation threatens, we begin with an affirmation of patience – that's the "wait" part. From here, we can begin the seeing – that is, the recognition of what is actual, what is true. Thus, "wait and see" are a trend of action, not a passive or static state. Seeing, to complete the progression, produces effective activity. Within the waiting and seeing mind-set, the path to solution becomes evident, whatever it may be. Perhaps you haven't noticed environmental factors, such as the sun or the wind, perhaps you need to smile and feel the breeze in your face, perhaps your actions are too quick, perhaps a speculation about results is causing fear. You will see. Seeing is knowing, and knowing produces action that is free from doubt.

Try This!

Experiment with the "wait and see" progression. Make it a training theme for one month. Be vigilant, and employ it as required, while, at the same time, noticing the factors that separate us from this natural and effective way of being. All methods, however wonderful, are stop-gap measures. The real work is to remove the conditions that make the methods necessary.

The power of human interest.

Seeing begins with looking, and looking comes naturally when there is *appreciation*. Life is so interesting, so beautiful, so filled with potential and wonder! This sincere, deep, heart-felt interest is foundational. It's the child-like quality that produces enthusiasm, and concentration is easy when we are enthused. Coaches are working with humans, and can we really define the limits of human potential? I don't think so. It is critical that one feel the magnificence of life. A truly noble approach is impossible without this sense of depth. The mind and heart and body of a human are capable of amazing feats, amazing grace, amazing beauty. Concentration, as a way of being, is simply a preoccupation with the discovery of this potential.

The reality of mind.

Concentration exercises, such as staring at a stationary ball for great lengths of time, or simply counting one's inhalations and/or exhalations (i.e. breathing exercises), are useful in many ways. Most people don't realize the scattered and undisciplined character of their thought processes. A few minutes of quiet breathing will quickly dispel such ignorance. How the mind wanders! Concentration exercises make the mind a real, concrete reality, which must be respected, studied and trained; we must cooperate with its functions.

Try This!

Always begin exercises, such as counting breaths, with serenity, stressing that concentration is something we allow, not something we force. If concentration wanders, patiently re-affirm the serenity, and then proceed.

Know thyself.

As we improve in our ability to focus the mind, we cease being the victim of our own thoughts and ideas. We discover that we actually have a say in what we think, or do not think; we can discriminate between the healthy and the unhealthy, the constructive and the destructive. This produces confidence, and provides a weapon against the wandering enemies of fear and doubt. Thus, when I'm about to serve and I hear that insidious voice that says, "don't double fault now," I'm aware of this suggestion, and can consciously let it go, using indignation, silence, humor and practical knowledge to dissolve the doubts. Thus, off-court work must be accompanied by on-court disciplines. It is wise, for instance, to begin every point with the mantra, "in the present, now, watch the ball," and to then review, after each point, whether the instruction was followed. As a junior I did this experiment for six months and was repeatedly amazed at how quickly I forgot the command, and how effective it was when I remembered.

The ultimate way.

Despite their obvious value, concentration exercises are actually of a probationary or introductory character. Eventually, with the overall defeat of fear and the attainment of sustained serenity, concentration becomes a way of life, a fact of who we are, and it thereby loses its character as a temporary resistance against various weaknesses. Thus, coaches, even while implementing concentration exercises, must place their emphasis upon enthusiasm and serenity, which, combined with fearlessness, make concentration natural and permanent. The aim is to *eliminate* fear and distraction, not to fight them. When the mind acts without fear as a spur, it's called meditation, and this meditative condition is synonymous with the zone. Concentration is the spring-board that takes us there.

Try This!

Introduce concentration as a way of being, a way of life, rather than a specialized skill that we apply only for the achievement of grandiose ambitions. Take the time to really look at a flower, to notice its shape, color and scent. Notice what players notice, and what they do not notice, and begin the work of expanding their degree of interest and attentiveness. Rearrange the objects in a room and see who notices. This is crucial for noble coaching and parenting, which seeks the blossoming of people, not just players. The idea is to integrate the noble qualities as features of who we are. In this realm, one leads by example, and also by creating or pointing out opportunities for interest in fascinating things.

NOBLE TENNIS
THE WISDOM OF SPORT

CHAPTER FIVE
Understanding Fear

NOBLE TENNIS
THE WISDOM OF SPORT

*At last we reach
The crux of the matter;
There's no more time
For chitter and chatter;*

*Dear reader,
Have you been glibly aloof,
Refusing to budge
Without "logical proof"?*

*There'll be no more of that,
Come enter the fray;
If we can't defeat fear,
There's nothing to say.*

*Not my fear, not your fear,
But fear as a whole;
The death of nobility,
The bain of the soul!*

*There's no need to panic,
It's not what you think -
Fear can be gone
From court, field and rink.*

*Yes fear is a lie,
It just isn't true;
It's all a bunch
of hullaballoo!*

*So examine yourself,
And see if I'm right;
There's no need to argue,
There's no need to fight;*

*Just give up the mind
That lustily seeks;
The ball's in your court -
fearlessness speaks!*

🍎 Questioning Common ideas 🍎

Dubious cliches.

There are a thousand cliches surrounding fear. Who hasn't heard the phrase, "fear is natural," or "fear is a good motivator"? But are these statements, which we repeat in a parrot-like fashion, actually true? I say they are false. Fear is not natural, in the sense of being unavoidable or necessary, and it is not a good motivator. On the contrary, fear is a bad, harmful motivator, and not fear but fearlessness deserves the highest praise. Where there is fear, there is no pure enthusiasm, nor serenity, nor patience, nor happiness, nor joy, nor the zone, nor etiquette, nor fair play and sportsmanship, nor ethics. Fear is the great bug-bear and spoiler of life; it must be understood, and dissolved.

Psychic Tylenol.

Today, there are countless gurus selling relief from fear. They make huge profits. Indeed, stress-busting is a giant industry! Relaxation, deep breathing, meditation, physical yoga, monastic retreats, tai chi and sport psychology share a common preoccupation with the alleviation of fear and anxiety. However, these practices, as currently advertised and taught, fail to reach the *causes* of fear, and are therefore just a patch-work of temporary remedies; they are to the psyche what Tylenol is to the body - useful, relieving, but not a cure. Hence, we must look deeper...

🍎 Defining Fear 🍎

The Fear Dynamic.

What is fear? It is a psychological or personal response to a set of stimuli or circumstances. Thus, there is nothing - no person, object or situation - that is *inherently* fearful, or scary; it's simply a question of how we see things. Therefore, it is conceivable to approach any situation without fear. Such fearlessness is our aim. In the absence of fear, enthusiasm and serenity find full scope, observation and intelligence are unimpeded, and the zone becomes a stable reality in life.

Fear is not "instinct."

There's a big difference between an instinctive recognition of danger and a fear reaction. If you place your finger near a hot element, the natural intelligence of the body impels you to remove it. That's a danger reaction, and its chief characteristic is spontaneous, automatic, intelligent activity. If you are subsequently terrified of all heat sources, that's a fear, and your actions will be faltering and irrational. Fear always produces stupidity, so it obviously has nothing to do with that natural intelligence whose instinctive responses are always appropriate to the situation. The conflation of instinct and fear is one of the great errors of modern thinking. Fear is a strictly human, or self-conscious phenomenon. It can only occur amongst those who have the ability to ponder the past and the future.

Try This!

Observe the workings of fear, and see whether it enhances harmony and intelligence, or whether it is their mortal enemy. The idea that fear is natural and valuable is very common, but is it right? Is the fear-fuelled world the best and only option we have? These are critical questions for sport, and for life.

The manufacturing sector.
Fear occurs when humans think their well-being is threatened. Fear, in other words, is *manufactured* by human thinking. This is very good news, for it means that fear can be noticed and addressed; it can be stopped, dissolved; we can close down the plant, and manufacture something else!

Fear, worry and tension.
The athlete sets up criteria for success, and then worries that these will not be met. This worry produces tension, and the athlete must now play through this tension, in spite of it. Sport becomes a form of resistance, something that is clumsy and ugly, lacking joy and rhythm. Surely, the production of such artificial anxieties and tensions is unnecessary, and unwise.

Try This!

It is wise to hold the phenomenon in the spotlight of the mind. Question your fears. Ask whether they are beneficial or not. We do that with almost everything else in life, so why not with psychological qualities? Write your fears down on paper – make them real, and then see if those fears can stand up to your reason and your courage. State alternatives to the fearful attitude and how an altered perspective will alter your actions and responses. These types of discussions can also take place in instructional settings, and if this means that the better part of a lesson is spent in discussion, do not regard it as something separate or superfluous. Many players and coaches think they're not teaching or learning if they aren't constantly "drilling," and parents often resent it when they see this "chit-chat" going on, but what's the use of all that physical work if fear can overtake you at any moment?

Origins of fear.
Where does fear come from? It comes from two words – "I want." If I want something to happen, I'm instantly aware that it might *not* happen. This negative, worrisome attitude towards the future produces fear. Fear, in other words, requires the desiring, coveting, lusting self; greed - obvious or subtle - is a precondition of fear.

A simple definition.
In the simplest terms: fear requires ambition, and ambition requires glamorous imaginings, or self-glorifying fantasies of the future – in a word, egoism. Fear requires speculation, and that peculiar blend of hope and dread which characterizes the undisciplined, fragmented, discontented mind.

The one and only fear.
There's really only one fear, and that's the fear of failure. All other fears fall under this broad umbrella: failure to survive (fear of death), failure to achieve, or receive, what one wants or needs (fear of want), failure to be appreciated or included (fear of humiliation, and/or isolation).

Athletic revolutionaries!
There are many popular synonyms for fear, and these flood the airwaves: stress, worry, anxiety, pressure, etc. These are all based in the negative, futuristic wanderings of the mind. If you look closely, you will discover that our whole society is founded on the cultivation of these speculative anxieties, based in desire and producing "the rat race." The perfect consumer is a desiring machine, driven by vanity, ambition and fear. Their existence is summarized in the phrase "I want, therefore I am," and they equate their every desire with an actual need - if they want it, they need

it. Every human problem and conflict – whether personal, familial, national or global; whether athletic, environmental, military, economic or political stems from this "I want" complex or structure. Thus, athletes who defeat fear are social revolutionaries, in a very deep and practical sense!

🍎 Fear In Action 🍎

The three reactions.

There are three reactions that indicate the presence of fear. These are called "fight," "flight" and "freeze." When athletes "freeze," it's often called "choking." This happens when the presence of fear causes such a contraction of the muscles that the proper execution of athletic actions is rendered impossible.

A "flight" reaction, within the context of sport, would involve an actual departure from the playing area, or, in more extreme cases, from the game itself. Indeed, many athletes experience a strong, almost desperate desire to "get the heck outta' here" when they're playing, and this feeling is a strong contributor to certain instances of "tanking" (i.e. when players stop trying, and more-or-less throw the match). This sense of wanting to vacate a fearful environment is actually quite appropriate. Some coaches will condemn these impulses as belonging to "losers" or "quitters," but this isn't always a proper assessment. Really, athletes are panicking because they are ignorant, and what they need is an understanding of the fears that have led to the unpleasant situation, so they can eliminate the misery from which they rightly want to escape. To expect players to "fight through it," without the key instruments of knowledge and understanding, is both cruel and unenlightened.

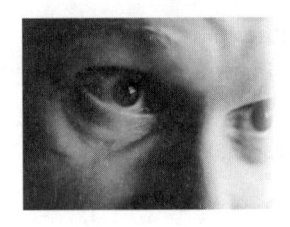

Try This!

Discuss fear frequently. See how it functions. A deep recognition of the absurdity and folly of fear is a crucial and potent element on the path to fearlessness. Of course, you may reject fearlessness as an option, but at least you'll be conscious of what you are doing and why. That's better than the "monkey see, monkey do" approach of most people today, who repeat cliches about fear without any reflection, and without any observation of their own experience.

A curious endorsement.

Players and coaches universally despise the freeze and flight reactions, but, strangely, they applaud and encourage the reaction called "fight." Athletes are instructed to develop the "eye of the tiger," to use nervousness and tension as allies, to cultivate a ruthlessness and grim determination through which they will act, violently, in spite of their fears, and win the match. Sport, in this case, is reduced to a form of resistance, and lacks the higher qualities that are felt and expressed in the zone.

Athletic pyromania.

When coaches support the "fight" approach, they're playing with an unwholesome and destructive fire. Players are asked to "manage" their fears, but can we be surprised when their attempts backfire, and the fear of failure elicits cheating, gamesmanship and violent fits of anger? It's irresponsible to release fear, with all its attendant calamities, into the world, when simple enthusiasm and serenity are open possibilities.

The path of fearlessness.

As a young player, I was encouraged - explicitly and implicitly - to develop "the fighting spirit." I was told "hate your opponent, be ruthless," but I couldn't do these things; it was against my nature, and I refused to alter myself in that direction. As a result, I became a temporary victim of fear. Unwilling to use fear as a stimulus, I waffled; I did the "freeze" reaction, and became a notorious under-achiever- a person who almost always "choked" at critical moments.

These were unhappy experiences, and I lost many matches to players I could have defeated. However, it was all for a good cause. Without knowing it at the time, for I was only a teenager, I was searching for an alternative to the "eye of the tiger" approach. I was innately aware of the ethical and qualitative dimensions of sport, and I wouldn't compromise these in the name of "winning." But this raised the question - is winning impossible without "ruthlessness?" I wasn't sure. And then, after years of enthusiastic technical, physical and psychological training, coupled with an increasing amount of study and exposure to a few excellent teachers, the fogs began to clear, and the path of fearlessness - the absence of fear - became a reality. In 1987, I played an entire tournament "in the zone." I, a high school student, defeated the entire starting line-up of the Queen's Varsity team, and I've never looked back. So, in the final analysis, the experiment was a success. Outer results came late, but they did come, and they came without gamesmanship or violence of any kind. It can be done! Through our own experiences and efforts, we can come to an understanding of fear, and fearlessness.

NOBLE TENNIS
THE WISDOM OF SPORT

Try This!

Realize that the whole world can be divided between those who think fear is necessary and those who strive for fearlessness. The latter may be in the minority, but does that make them wrong? You must think and see for yourself. If you accept fear, then the wisdom of sport and the qualitative approach are not for you.

NOBLE TENNIS
THE WISDOM OF SPORT

CHAPTER SIX
Fearlessness

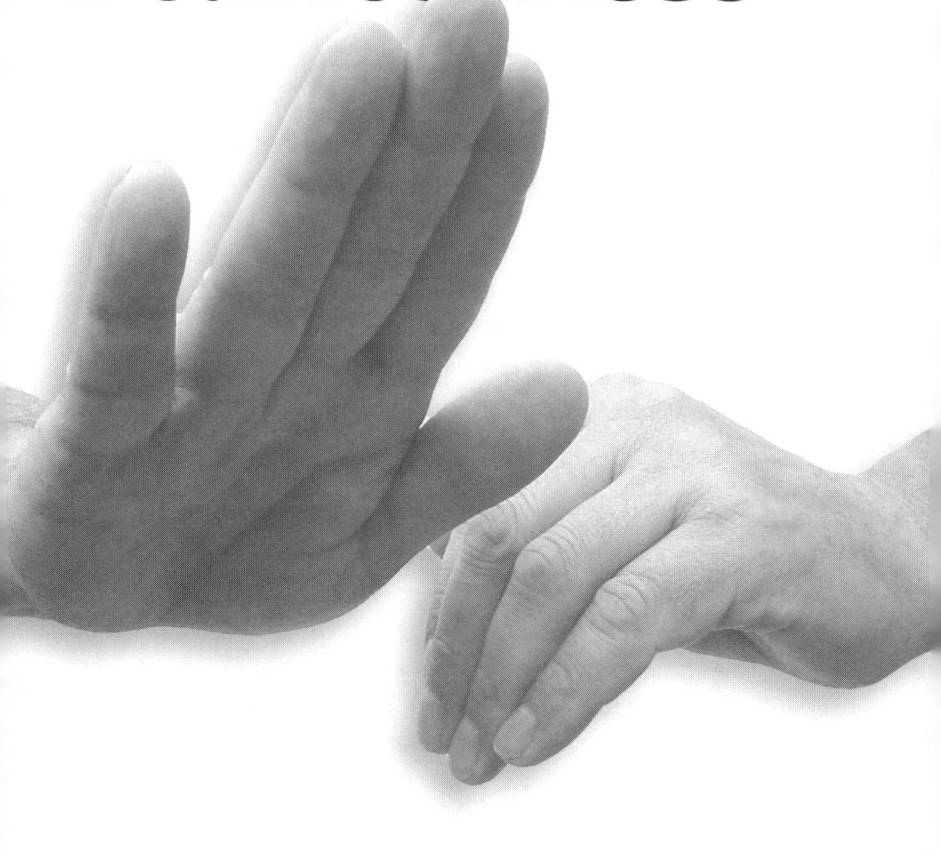

The weakness of toughness.
The elimination of fear isn't a form of resistance. As long as one feels the need to be "mentally tough" - to fight fear, or use fear, or even defeat fear, the real victory and the deep understanding has not been attained, nor will it ever be attained through such means. Even if a "ruthless competitor" successfully suppresses fear, or "channels" fear, it's only a momentary achievement. Fearlessness doesn't mean acting in spite of fear (that's called courage); it means acting in the *absence of fear*. The two are very different. Where fear ends, the zone begins.

🍎 Foundations of fearlessness 🍎

The ultimate solution.
What, then, is the ultimate solution to fear? Well, we've seen that fear is generated through expectation and speculation, so it follows that fear ends when we stop wanting, and stop speculating. Does this sound odd, or unrealistic? It isn't. It's precisely what happens in the zone. The player who has achieved the noble zone has ceased thinking about their sport. Instead, they are completely absorbed in the sport.

I am.
What we experience in the zone is a transformation of consciousness. It's not just the playing that changes; it's the player. Indeed, the one follows from the other. At the most fundamental level, this transformation involves a new and different feeling about who and what we are. The mind-set that says "I want" is replaced with the deep feeling of "I am." The "I want" individual feels somehow incomplete, inadequate, insecure. They feel the need to add something to who they are, and they think this will happen if they can win things, get things. This is very juvenile,

adolescent. The "I am" person, on the other hand, proceeds from a feeling of stability and serenity; they proceed from a basic position of strength. This does not make them arrogant or lazy. No, it just imbues striving with fearlessness and joy. It ensures sportsmanship, or ethical conduct, and it allows one to remain calm and supple, thereby releasing the best possibilities.

Try This!

Actively replace the thought "I want, so I play", with the thought "I am, and I play." Mantras like this are effective, and they can be developed or expanded in accordance with the intuition of each person. Fear begins with a thought that embodies a perspective. Change the thought and you change everything.

Interest motivates.

Immediately the objection will come: what motivates the noble player, if not the desire for an outcome, such as winning? The response is simple: interest motivates. Tennis, like life, is infinitely interesting – there is so much to observe, so many heights to be scaled, so much work to be done, so much learning to accomplish! If you look behind this interest, you might find a natural, innate urge to grow, to refine, to perfect, to blossom. I call this urge, "pure enthusiasm." But this enthusiasm is not an ambition, formulated out of arbitrary desires. On the contrary, it is the expression of an evolutionary urge that moves everything – from a flower to a human being - along. In the zone, we feel we are *participating* in a movement that is natural and powerful, and it has nothing to do with what we "want" to occur. Wanting is always followed by attempts to control and manipulate, but this is the end of co-creative participation.

NOBLE TENNIS
THE WISDOM OF SPORT

Try This!

Make it clear that fear is the one thing that must not motivate our actions. Encourage players to become sensitive to the types of environment that promote fear, such as tournaments, and the types of thought that act as trigger mechanisms for the onset of fear. Remind student's that they can respond to the first whiff of fear. Do not pretend it's not there, thereby allowing it to grow and develop to bigger and bigger proportions. Fear motivation can be replaced with motivation by interest.

Pseudo god is dead!

In the zone, we become a force of nature, not a pseudo-god that tries, but fails, to stand above nature, manipulating and controlling in accordance with "personal goals" and "child-hood dreams." In the zone, we feel a sense of freedom from the tiny world of ambitions, hopes and fears that constitute our "normal" existence; the speculating mind, the agent of our puny concerns, is silent, and this makes the noble zone a truly innocent place. Thus, the noble player works and strives, like a lily of the field, and who can deny the power of the mysterious engine that moves that process along, allowing beauty to unfold?

A precise formula.

There's an old saying: "when you don't want it, you can have it." In this so-called cliché is contained the entire secret of fearlessness, and the zone; it's a precise formula, whose validity is confirmed by countless examples, drawn from actual, common occurrences. Consider, for example, the following tennis scenario: Frank is receiving Jenny's serve. Jenny's first serve is improperly struck, and it soon becomes clear that it's going long (i.e. beyond the service line, or boundary). Seeing this, Frank relaxes, calls the serve "out" and swings his racquet, almost lazily, at the oncoming ball. As a result of this relaxed, un-self-conscious motion, he hits a blazing shot, right down the line!

What has happened here? In the instant when Frank recognizes that the ball's going out, and that it therefore has no bearing on the outcome of the match, from a competitive, statistical point of view, he's released from wanting, with its attendant anxieties. Hence, he is *free* from that which inhibits the execution of a proper stroke, and the resulting shot is a reflection of this liberation. Normally, Frank will *want* to reproduce his previous shot, and he will thereby re-introduce speculation and expectation into his tennis. As a result, he will probably flub the next return, even though he's receiving a second serve, which is softer than the first. Ah, the tyranny and the travesty of fear!

The mind of the beginner.

When we understand ambitious wanting as the source of fear, we can see the natural, scientific basis for "beginner's luck." The beginner doesn't "expect" to succeed. This means they are free from speculation, and this allows them to perform actions with the innocence and fearless enthusiasm that lead to the best results. It's really quite simple, don't you think? In the zone, we are all beginners - people who have no selfish expectations or preconceived notions about what we can or cannot achieve.

Attaining Fearlessness

Fear and competition.

Fear can't be eliminated if we fail to address materialism and competitiveness. A competitive attitude, or outlook, is a breeding ground for fear. In the mind of the competitor, the world consists of winners and losers, haves and have-nots. The goal of the competitor is to be amongst the winners - an aspiration that gives full scope to the fear of failure. Under the influence of this ambition, other people are seen as enemies, since one person's gain must be another's loss, and vice-versa. Hence, violence and paranoia (i.e. fight and flight - fear) are inherent within the competitive attitude. That's a problem.

Fear and materialism.

The fear of the competitor is heightened when the rewards of sport are seen from a materialistic point of view, such as exists everywhere today. There are only so many top rankings, or scholarships, or prizes to go 'round, so we must want these things very badly, we must dream of them incessantly, we must pursue them like a lion after its prey. In this paragraph is summarized the neurosis of modern times.

Useless pastimes.

Competitiveness and materialism are wastes of energy. The materialistic competitor lives in a fantasy-land of hopes and fears. To what end? What is gained thereby? It is crucial to realize the illusory and useless character of the world of speculation, the world of "what if?" Why build prisons for yourself? Why prescribe limits? Your task, from the perspective of the wisdom of sport, is to focus all your interest on the actual, the here and now, the realm of real growth and real learning. This will require discipline, especially in the early phases, and especially at tournaments, competitions, whose primary function is to test our ability to remain centered and interested at all times.

A greater enterprise.

The wisdom approach to sport does not imply that competitions and prizes should be outlawed, banished, or rejected. Instead, it suggests that we must develop a proper attitude in relation to these things, so they don't rule our lives and breed destructive fear. There's nothing *inherently* wrong with contests or prizes, but they must be seen as aspects of a much greater enterprise, whose themes are cooperation, perfectment and qualitative excellence. In this context, contests are stimulating, fun, educational, and prizes are signs of appreciation and recognition. There's nothing harmful in that.

Try This!

Discuss the attitude that revels in freedom from the snares of competitiveness and materialism. Perhaps watch films or read books about great heroes who have lived free from the pettiness and fear that these preoccupations breed. The film "Chariots of Fire" is brilliant in this respect. Eric Liddel represents the free man, while Harold Abrams represents the one who is struggling with ambition, pride and fear. Also, I would recommend the films "Little Buddha," "Phenomenon" and "Searching for Bobby Fisher." It is crucial that people discover people by whom they can be inspired to fearlessness, and who point to the truly significant thing, which is human potential.

The "normal" is not the best.

Now we can see why popular remedies for fear don't work. The *elimination* of fear requires *an approach to life* that runs totally counter to what's called "normal" in the modern world. The alternative to the "normal" is the qualitative approach, which is the polar opposite of the competitive and materialistic. The noble athlete experiences an *inward* striving that is completely independent of material aims and outcomes. To the casual observer, such a player will seem competitive, because they bring one hundred per cent of themselves to every point, every moment, every action. But the *source* of their efforts is entirely different from the norm, and this difference will be obvious to the sensitive viewer. There will be a peace, a joy, a pervasive quality of nobility that will shine through the outer play. Andre Agassi, when he miraculously won Wimbledon, seemed to be expressing these qualities. In this world of enthusiastic, concentrated striving, there's no such thing as failure, and when one succeeds, we all succeed. After all, how can anyone be worse off when the higher qualities of a human being are cultivated and expressed?

Try This!

Realize that fearlessness is evolved in and through living relationships. Life itself presents opportunities to address fear. We cannot do it artificially. Our task is to understand fear and fearlessness, and to apply this understanding in life. Thus, fearlessness must become an important theme in your thinking and observing. When this occurs, it will cross your mind to deal with things at this level, and you will become vigilant, sensitive and effective.

A call to leadership.
Coaches and parents must lead the way in making these attitudes and techniques practical. No word should be uttered that's based in fear, or which could produce fear. Indeed, coaches and parents should radiate fearlessness. They should impress their students and children with the understanding that outward results are secondary, and that if they attend to the inner conditions, if they train hard, the best results will flow naturally and effortlessly, like an unimpeded stream.

The synthesis of the qualities.
Fearlessness occurs every time we experience any of the basic qualities and virtues. In concentration, for instance, time disappears. There is no past, and no future; there is only now. Under these circumstances, there can be no wanting, no longing, no speculating. Thus, the *sources* of fear - egotistical speculation and expectation - *do not exist* when we concentrate, and, as a result, fear can't get a foothold in the mind. Serenity is what fearlessness feels like in the heart and mind and body, and the active joy of this fearless absorption is called pure enthusiasm. Hence, when we accept and implement the qualitative approach to sport, we are on the path that leads to fearlessness.

Fear Antidotes

The garden of the mind.
Fear and doubt invade the mind. Like a virus, or a weed, they spread. The voice of fear has been compared to a "dark whisperer," like the little cartoon devil that sits on your shoulder and suggests horrible things. Coaches, therefore, must encourage players to become increasingly aware of their own thoughts and feelings, so they can respond appropriately to intruding ideas of a negative

character. Ask your students to take you through a game or a match, *at the level of thought*. What occurred to them? How did they respond? What were the effects? This will be especially important during the early stages of qualitative training. Ultimately, we can become like a garden that's more-or-less immune to weeds, but, in the meantime, we must be vigilant.

The sense of humor.

When confronted by a fearful suggestion, there are several lines of thinking and feeling that act like powerful antidotes. These should be known by everyone. Thus, for instance, we can employ the sense of humor. Fear makes little things seem like big things. When you recognize the ultimate irrelevance of the outcome of a single match or game, when seen within the broad context of life and happiness, you might be inclined to chuckle. This represents an appropriate belittling of the fearful suggestion, and it thereby loses its power. It's like a child who discovers the monster in their closet was really just a distorted image of their own clothing: we feel a little silly about our extravagant speculations and dramatic reactions!

The breakfast solution.

Once, I coached a player who was prone to fits of anger and frustration, based, as always, in fear. One day, when he was struggling, I stopped the drill and said "so what did you have for breakfast this morning?" This question, which was so out of place, had a transforming effect. The player burst out laughing, and we proceeded to enjoy ourselves and make progress. Fear is a fixation upon something that's been blown out of proportion. Restore the proportion, and you restore sanity.

Solemnity.

When the fearful thoughts are persistent, then a response of solemnity might be required. Such a solemn reaction is wonderfully demonstrated in the film "Patton," which outlines the military career of this famous American general. In one scene, Patton's headquarters are bombed by enemy planes. Initially, he hides under a table - a natural, danger response, but when the planes continue to fly back and forth, dropping their bombs, he suddenly exclaims "by God - that's enough!" At this point, he runs into the street, fires his pistol at the planes and dares them to shoot him "right in the nose!" In that instant, Patton affirms that *anything* would be better than a continued cowering underneath his desk; he has said "no!" to fear, *regardless* of the circumstances, or the outcome. Such a powerful and unequivocal affirmation captures the essence of solemnity. Solemnity is a proper pride, or arrogance; it's the audacity to declare your stature as a free, dignified, responsible, fearless being.

The Patton solution.

Fear, and the circumstances that surround it, will yield to a sincere, solemn declaration. There have been several occasions - usually in tournament matches when I'm playing with tension and anxiety - when I've recalled this scene from Patton, and been inspired by it. The results have been superb. Solemnity means that a person will "play their game," no matter what. And isn't this common-sensical? After all, how else can we perform our task with joy and effectiveness?

Knowledge.

Also, coaches need to realize the relationship between fear and ignorance. Players will panic if they are unable to understand or escape from their own errors. Hence, when practicing, it's wise to have the player explain what they do well or poorly in various instances. The coach can verify these assertions, or make corrections and offer alternative explanations. Then, when the player is struggling, they will have the technical information and the mental wherewithal to observe, think, and make their own adjustments.

The vast middle ground.

Recently, I was working with a young player on his serve, and I asked him to demonstrate how he intended to hit the stroke in an upcoming tournament. This he did, and the result was rather alarming - the serve he showed me was a mere shadow of his actual capabilities, and it bore no resemblance to what we'd been practicing; it was weak, it lacked spin and it was shallow. When I asked why he planned to hit the serve this way, he explained that he would probably be *afraid* to miss it in the tournament, so he'd make it weak, but consistent. When I asked if he thought it was good to be afraid, he said yes, because it stopped him from trying wild, low percentage shots.

I responded to these comments by clarifying what they really implied; namely, that he was a very stupid person when he wasn't afraid! A person who would be thoughtless and wild if he wasn't afraid! I asked if it was possible to be unafraid, and yet very intelligent. He said yes, and we came to the realization that between the two extremes of fear and stupidity there's a vast middle ground, and that ground is called knowledge. He recognized that he *knew* how to hit the serve properly, and, if he did miss it, he was capable of making corrections. Thus, knowledge, when applied, leads to confidence, and fear cannot survive in such a setting.

Try This!

Make experiments. Go to a tournament and make fearlessness via solemnity, humor or applied knowledge the sole or dominant theme. Later, this can be branched out, and the player can intuit which of these responses is most apt. Eventually, this artificiality will not be necessary at all. We must remember that fearlessness is possible, so the need for antidotes indicates incomplete attainment. Fear is something we leave behind; we forget about it. This forgetting cannot occur if we are unduly preoccupied with battling fear as a problem. The emphasis needs to be on enthusiasm and serenity. That way, fear will be something we notice, but not something we actively attract. The work of replacing "I want" with "I am" represents the creation of an environment that does not attract, or produce, fear.

Closing the gap.

Yes, coaches must address the gap between what is done in practice and what is done in tournaments, or actual games. The space between is where fear enters. Thus, when I take kids to a tournament, I explain that the only failure is the failure to think, enjoy, and play full-out. I explain that all our training is a complete waste of time if they respect their fears more than their love of the game, and their coach! Their task, I sometimes say, is to please me, and they do this if they apply what they've learned to the best of their ability. In this way, I seek to introduce a force more powerful than the fears that attack and belittle. A coach is a beacon of fearlessness, and it's okay to affirm oneself as a center of inspiration, when the motive is selfless and uplifting.

Mature watching.

The way a person watches a match is very important. In the past, parents have been surprised to observe how I often sit completely upright and still, with an expression of total calmness on my face. At such times I am consciously embodying the energies of serenity and fearlessness, in support of the players. Negative gesturing, sarcastic or mean remarks, and even unduly "positive" gesticulations strike me as very inappropriate, and quite immature.

A transformation.

A sense of humor, a broad perspective, solemnity and knowledge are all effective when confronted by fear, but the ultimate solution lies at a deeper level. The achievement of a stabilized fearlessness requires a transformation of perspective. But believe me, it's worth it! The transformation that eliminates fear is a transition from the combativeness of the competitive attitude to the unquenchable striving of simple enthusiasm; from the quantitative realm into the qualitative. This essential change of mind involves a willingness to take that "leap of faith" through which we stop speculating about results, stop forming fears and ambitions, stop, as a friend of mine says, "being so damned selfish," and live simply, enthusiastically and patiently within the flow of the present, letting things unfold as they will. As the great Taoist Sage Chuang Tzu says, "so then, flow with whatever may happen and let your mind be free; stay centered by accepting whatever you are doing. This is the ultimate. How else can you carry out your task? It is best to leave everything to work naturally, though this is not easy." The ability to live and play in this manner is the enduring gift of the athletic enterprise. The lesson of sport is fearlessness, and the reward of sport is effortless grace, or beauty.

NOBLE TENNIS
THE WISDOM OF SPORT

CHAPTER SEVEN
The Inner Life

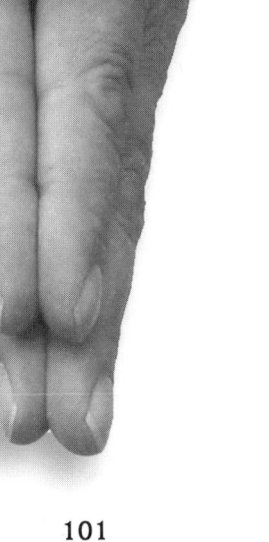

The proper ratio.

Napoleon said, "the mind is to the body as one hundred is to one." I think this idea is worth pondering! Indeed, his statement needs to be taken literally. Chiefly, the power of thoughts and feelings must be recognized.

🍎 Mind-Body Relations 🍎

Interactive energies.

How do thoughts and physical states interact? Modern science suggests that all that exists is energy in motion. This applies to the body - which is actually a configuration of energy fields - and also to thoughts and feelings. Hence, thoughts and bodies can inter-act because they're both forms of energy. When a thought occurs, it effects the electro-magnetic energy that constitutes the body, with its various systems, organs, tissues, etc. Thus, every thought and feeling impacts the body, thereby producing chemical and biological effects. This can also work in reverse: physical inputs, like food and drink, are capable of influencing patterns of thinking and feeling. However, while the psyche is capable of being influenced by physical inputs, and while these should definitely be regulated with care, it isn't necessarily so. A strong psyche will remain relatively unchanged, if it so wills, in spite of physical pressures; but the body will inevitably respond to psychic factors, so these must be watched with even greater attention.

Try This!

Take seriously the Tennis Canada injunction to observe the psychological first. Practice this. Most coaches simply lack comfort and familiarity with the psychological life, so the technical and tactical win by default. However with knowledge of the indispensable qualities herein outlined, the situation can change. There is no excuse now, and continued neglect of the critical issues at hand will be the result strictly of laziness, habit, and prejudice.

Two formulas.

The above ideas can be summarized in the simple phrases, *all is energy* and *energy follows thought*. These constitute a formula that can revolutionize your understanding of many things, including athletic training. I invite you to ponder them, and test their validity.

The body obeys.

The power of the psyche is constantly demonstrated. Consider, for example, the following tennis scenario: John is serving at 5-5 in the deciding set of a match. The score is 30-40, break point, and John is about to hit a second serve. As he prepares to do so, he suddenly has a thought - "double fault." The body receives the energy of this thought and responds appropriately: the muscles tighten, the heart beats faster (because of the fear contained in the thought), physical balance and rhythm are diminished. In doing these things the body is simply adapting to, or following, the thought; it sets into motion the physical states required to fulfill the idea, thereby proving the partial validity of the old cliché, "life is a self-fulfilling prophecy."

Try This!

Play practice matches during which the player, at change-overs, has to define what has occurred at the level of thought. They may find this difficult in the beginning. They will be inclined to tell you what physically happened, but this isn't really what you're after. Thus, you will need to clarify that what you're asking is if any thoughts or ideas occurred to them as they played, keeping in mind that the observation of total mental silence is perfectly valid, though quite unusual.

Another example.

Or, here's another example: It was spring-time, and I thought I'd better do some jogging to prepare myself for the rigors of the upcoming summer season. It had been a long winter of studying and writing, and my physical conditioning wasn't quite up to par, or so I thought. So out I went. On the day I have in mind, things weren't going very well. My breathing was irregular, and I was beginning to cramp. My mind was filled with thoughts, and I was preoccupied with looking at my watch to check my pace, and to see how much longer before I could stop. It was most unpleasant. Then it hit me: "Tony," something said, "stop this! This is juvenile – beneath you." I heard this like a load-lifting command. I kept jogging, but I turned off the stop-watch. I began to look at the trees and feel the wind in my face. The cramp was gone, the facial muscles relaxed, the breathing was rhythmic. I no longer "wanted" to run for a certain amount of time, I no longer "wanted" to be fit. I could have kept going indefinitely. The "inner" had changed, and the outer responded instantly and completely, with full obedience.

Try This!

Keep a log of psychological observations and experiences. Don't rely on so-called experts – perform your own experiments! You are the experiment, and the experimenter.

Mixed messages.

Most people are unclear in their thinking and feeling. We have "mixed emotions" about almost everything, so our thoughts are fragmentary and confused. As a result, the body is constantly receiving mixed messages, and this causes great inefficiency. The body is an adapting mechanism, and a very good one, as millions of years of physical evolution prove, but, when the environment lacks consistency, the adaptive process is very difficult. The polar bear is perfectly suited to life in the arctic, but it couldn't have survived, or would have developed very differently, if the arctic went through radical changes every five years! So, imagine how the body feels, as it tries to adapt to the thousands of thoughts - often contradictory - that most people think in a day!

An unacknowledged power.

In short, players and coaches must realize the power of

suggestion. Often, when faced with the power of thought, people say, "it's just a placebo." What an absurd statement! How can we say, *just* a placebo? Do we mean, just the power of psychic states to alter physical ones? This power should be seriously investigated, not shrugged off as though it were nothing! When mothers lift giant trees off their children, is that "just a placebo?" When patients recover fifty per cent faster in hospitals that show kindness and attention to the soothingness of the environment, is that "just a placebo?" When athletic contests are won and lost on the basis of "attitude," is that "just a placebo?" When whole historical epochs are shaped and guided by ideas that effect people's thinking - is that "just a placebo?" Indeed, "placebo" is everywhere, and we'll all be better off when the power of suggestion is understood, and when we learn how to develop and regulate our psychological capacities. Athletic training offers a relatively harmless medium for such investigations.

🍎 Intelligent Work 🍎

The first step.

Given the power of thought, one of the first tasks of the player will be to quiet the mind, and to exert a conscious influence over which psychological inputs are accepted, and which are rejected. Clarity is the aim. This requires an examination of principles and motives, since these form the foundation of all thought processes. Part of John, our server, is ruthlessly competitive, and wants to win at all costs, while, at the same time, he realizes "winning isn't everything" and "it's the effort that counts." Thus, there are opposing ideas within John, and he must choose between them if he wants to be mentally consistent and physically efficient.

People, in other words, must come to a conscious realization of what they are doing, and why. This is the first step towards maturity, as well as efficiency and quality in physical training.

Try This!

Do exercises of mindfulness. For instance, try to go through one full day, or perhaps one hour, with a complete sense of what you are doing and why. Imagine – a day in full-waking consciousness, with little or no mental automatism, or merely conditioned routine.

Mental programs.

Once we recognize the power of thought and suggestion, we also discover the need to notice mental patterns or "programs." A pattern of thought, once established, becomes an automatic response to specific situations. When such mental patterns are harmful, we need to do a little de-programming. How does this work? Consider, for example, the following: I recently played in a doubles tournament. My partner and I reached the final, and were involved in a close match. We were trailing 5-4 in the first set, and it was my turn to serve. As I stepped to the line, I was assaulted by a feeling of doubt. The presence of this doubt produced a sense of "pressure," and this inhibited my play. On the first point, I hit a double fault. Soon we were down 15-40, double set point. At this stage, I suddenly realized that I was running a mental program. I, the conscious, alive, alert person, was no longer present; there was only an old pattern that had been clicked into gear. My response to this realization was simple and effective. I said to myself – "no, I'm not running that program again." At this point, I had a spontaneous visualization of a finger pressing the stop button on a recording machine. My mind was silent. I hit my serve with ease, moved with balance to the net and executed a difficult volley. We won the point. At 30-40, fearlessness allowed me to hit an ace on a second serve, and we had soon won the game and the set, 7-5.

In the days that followed, I became aware of the many programs that ran themselves in my day-to-day life, and I also recognized that they could always be stopped, dissolved, ended. There is no need to exchange one program for another. The goal is not the production of a "positive self-image." On the contrary, the goal is no-goal; the goal is full-waking consciousness, or complete presence of mind, total attention, utter aliveness. This does not imply that we constantly "decide" what to do. On the contrary, complete enthusiasm and concentration, within an atmosphere of serenity and patience, releases a natural, spontaneous Intelligence that is far more effective than any image we can muster. Our responsibility is to create an environment in which this Intelligence can operate. When we do, all our best accumulations of skill and experience are naturally employed.

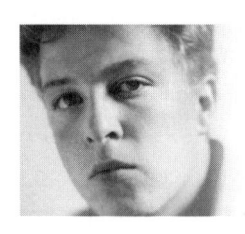

Try This!

Further exercises in mindfulness: say a "mantra" or phrase before each point; have players call out ball characteristics or appropriate shot selections during drills; ask questions to see who notices different things in the environment. True, all of this is unnecessary in the zone, but the concentration of mindfulness is the spring-board that takes us there. It is preparatory work.

The greater issue.

So far we've considered only self-centered reasons for respecting the power of suggestion, but we should also realize that the impact of our thoughts and feelings isn't limited to our own physical bodies. Human beings aren't separate islands, living in private worlds. On the contrary, all things are connected. My thoughts effect my body, to be sure, but they also radiate out into the greater environment, like radio-waves. If a sensitive person walks into a room filled with angry people, they will instantly recognize that something's wrong. Such a recognition doesn't require an observation of facial expressions, or gestures of any kind; these are just supportive evidence. No, you will feel the energy of the environment, even before you observe it. Indeed, the people in the room might try to mask what's been happening, through a superficial politeness, but it won't work. Thus, it's undeniable that *people create environments*, and the importance of this, especially for parents and coaches, should be quite obvious - create an environment of fear and ambition, and you will evoke meanness and greed; create one of serene enthusiasm, and the results will be very, very different.

The work to be done.

Thus, we return once again to the power of suggestion. Each of us lives in a world filled with suggestions. Today, this poses a particularly important problem, since most of the suggestions in our environment – e.g. those that come to us through television and other mass media - are based on and produce speculation, fear, doubt and worry. Or, to take another example, tournaments – these are veritable hot-beds of negative suggestion. It is crucial that these suggestions don't stick. We must be utterly unresponsive in this direction. This can only happen if we are deeply interested in pursuing the path of nobility. Saying "no" to one thing requires a "yes" to something else. The "no" and the "yes" are your responsibility. Most of us are too yielding, too willing to adapt to all the suggestions that come to us. The path of nobility begins when we become dissatisfied with our conditioning, with the programs that we faithfully run, without noticing or questioning. The work of the noble player is to dissolve these programs, and learn to be fully awake, fully aware, fully alive. This occurs as we become interested in the noble qualities, and increasingly aware of the Intelligence that arrives when all speculations, expectations and images have been stilled.

Try This!

Endeavour to root out the unspoken assumptions and ideas that motivate players, and then examine whether they are constructive or not. This occurs easily when you ask questions – especially that master of all questions: why?, listen, and clarify the ideas that are being expressed. This can occur in off-court discussions, or it can be ignited by on-court situations, as they arise.

🍎 Inner Development 🍎

Creative intelligence.
There are three main types of thought. First, there are those that emanate from the "I want" complex. These thoughts are speculative, and tinged with fear, doubt and general dis-ease. They

are the source of every human vice, as the separate individual proclaims his right to do and get whatever he or she wants. Almost all the suggestions in modern life appeal to this mind.

Second, there are thoughts of a purely technical variety. These are absolutely necessary for day-to-day life. They help us to plan, organize, and generally get from A to B. This form of thought is applied on the tennis court when we focus on one or two very specific elements, and also when we undertake things like periodized planning. It is widely considered the practical instrument of the "I want" complex. Technical thought isn't necessarily harmful, but we run into trouble when we think it's the only mind we've got.

Third, there's creative thought. The recognition and development of this aspect of mind is what tennis, which is a creative activity, is all about. The thinking of this mind is completely different from the previous two. It occurs when the "I want" mind is completely silent. This level of thought, which is so difficult to describe in normal language, has many names – "the Higher Self," "the Tao," etc. I simply call it Creative Intelligence. "The zone" is the term that applies to life when it is lived under the influence of this Creative Intelligence.

Try This!

Get to know the three varieties or aspects of mind. What mind generally defines you? Which are you using now? Are you an isolated individual, fighting to get what you want? Are you a walking brain – an analyzing machine? Or are you an intelligence that's connected with a Greater Intelligence, one that has meaning and purpose in and of itself? When you meet a person, a new student perhaps, observe what kind of mind they bring. Make experiments. Run three practices, using the three different varieties of mind as the guiding principle. Note the responses of yourself and your students. Recall, when doing this, that the "I want" mind appeals to selfish ambition, will use fear as a motivator, and gets everyone "pumped!" The technical mind appeals to the sense of prudence and systematic method. The Creative mind brings an intense, calm strength and joy, plus a passion for life and sport. It is intensely observant, open, and contains an element that the other two minds tend to lack – humour. I suggest that the individualistic and technical aspects of mind only function properly when under the influence of the Creative. This Creative mind is synonymous with the zone, and is hence the critical factor in both practice and competitive settings. But what does it matter what I say? It's for you to try, and see.

A step forward.

The depth, variety and intensity of the inner life, the life of thoughts and feelings, varies from person to person. Often, the most successful athletes are those with a relatively undeveloped thought-life. They are able to play with a high degree of calmness, mainly because there are few psychological elements to be ordered and harmonized. For example, I remember one person who, as a junior, was known throughout the province for his icy composure and his consistent ability to win decisive points. He never choked. Indeed, I myself lost several close matches to this quiet guy, and witnessed his remarkable attributes in action.

Years later I ran into him at an open, adult tournament. He had just lost a rather uninspired match and was sitting in the lounge, reading a book on sport psychology. We started talking, and I eventually asked him about his junior career – what methods, if any, did he use? How was it that he never choked? His response was very illuminating. Basically, he said he never choked because he never thought. He was practically an automaton. He trained his body, and his mind was pretty much a non-factor. In the past few years, he explained, his tennis had suffered, and it was all because he had begun to think. He no longer "just did it." Instead, he wanted to know why he was doing it, and his thinking was making him nervous and uncertain when he played. He had developed a temper, and was certainly not enjoying himself. He knew that he could not reverse the basic situation – he could not go backwards to the time when thought was a non-issue. Hence, the book on sport psychology.

In responding to these insights, I simply assured him that, despite all appearances, this was a move forward, not backward, and I said I would get on with finishing my book, which might be of interest!

Rejecting Pavlov.

So, should the unthinking automaton be our model? A lot of people seem to think so. Certainly, this was the view that inspired the Soviet Bloc of bygone days, and they were enormously successful at the level of "performance" and "results." But the Wisdom rejects and actually reverses this approach to sport. It aims at the growth and development of human beings, as human beings. As this growth occurs we become increasingly rich, variegated, abundant, diverse. Our task, then, is two-fold: first, we do the work of constantly growing, learning, expanding in terms of experience and understanding. Second, and at the same time, we incorporate all this material into a unity, a harmony, a single orchestra of many instruments. This harmony is achieved with great facility when the noble qualities are functioning as constant variables. Think back to the first paragraph of the first chapter of this book: "the keynote of sport is harmony." The more we have to harmonize, the more interesting and challenging the work, and also the more magnificent the result, when achieved.

Passion.

Inner maturity does not involve a lack of feeling, or passion, or aspiration. On the contrary, Creative Intelligence is inspired intelligence. The main question is this: what inspires joy? Joy is the elevation of the feeling nature. It is feeling that is free from fear. Hence, we can never know joy from within the "I want" complex, because it is always tinged with fear. The happiness of the competitor consists largely in a sense of relief that their worst fears were not realized. This seems a rather paltry thing, a low pinnacle! However, pure enthusiasm is an essentially joyous state. To be deeply involved in what one is doing, to care about it without being afraid, to savor the feeling of rhythm and timing and general competence, to aspire endlessly into perfectment, to feel the thrill of learning and improving, to appreciate the miracle of being human, and all the wonders of this world, this is the refinement and maturation of feeling.

Try This!

In all your coaching and parenting, encourage and applaud insight, observation, and understanding. Demonstrate and encourage fine and noble feelings. Teach kids to revel in the playing of the game, and in the striving to mastery. This expansion of understanding and refinement of feeling is what it means to be a living, growing, maturing human being. We are not computers or slabs of meat to be simply "trained" and "drilled" and "programmed." If you can feel and know this, then you are on the path of the wisdom of sport.

The required intensity.

Only a passionate interest in the noble way can ensure that all the snags and distractions will be overcome. It is crucial to feel a deep, passionate repulsion in relation to the ugly and the juvenile. The work of maturing is not for spaced-out lotus-landers. It requires vigilance, and commitment. You will face a barrage of opposing ideas and forces. But your attraction to the greater possibilities of life and sport will take you past all obstacles.

What lies ahead.

Thus, an infantile automatism is not the way. Such an approach focuses on "efficiency" and outer results at the expense of human maturation. That is unacceptable. The qualitative approach, on the other hand, stresses that human maturation is the critical result, and outer results are just that – results, effects, things that "just happen." Now you can see why I said my friend at the tournament had taken a step forward. He had moved from unthinking automatism to confused thought. Hence, his life had been broadened by a new, powerful and interesting factor. The fact that the presence of this new factor was disruptive says nothing against it. Growth is the crucial thing, and crises are absolutely essential for growth. "Comfort," they say, "is the cemetery of the spirit," and "every crisis is an opportunity." True. What my friend experienced was the perfectly natural growth from the childish to the adolescent stage of development. The child is untroubled by thought. The adolescent is tortured by it. The task of the adolescent is to become familiar with thought, to learn how it

NOBLE TENNIS
THE WISDOM OF SPORT

functions, and to incorporate thought into the structure of his life. That is the path to maturity. When that incorporation occurs he will once again play with calmness and composure, but now it will be different, because understanding will be included, thereby multiplying the joy and beauty of the endeavor. Thought will no longer be speculation, it will not be allied with fear; the voice of "I want!" will be still; the control-mania of analysis will be non-existent; observation will replace these harmful modes of thought, and he will become an active participant in his ever-evolving perfectment. That is what lies ahead for the noble athlete.

NOBLE TENNIS
THE WISDOM OF SPORT

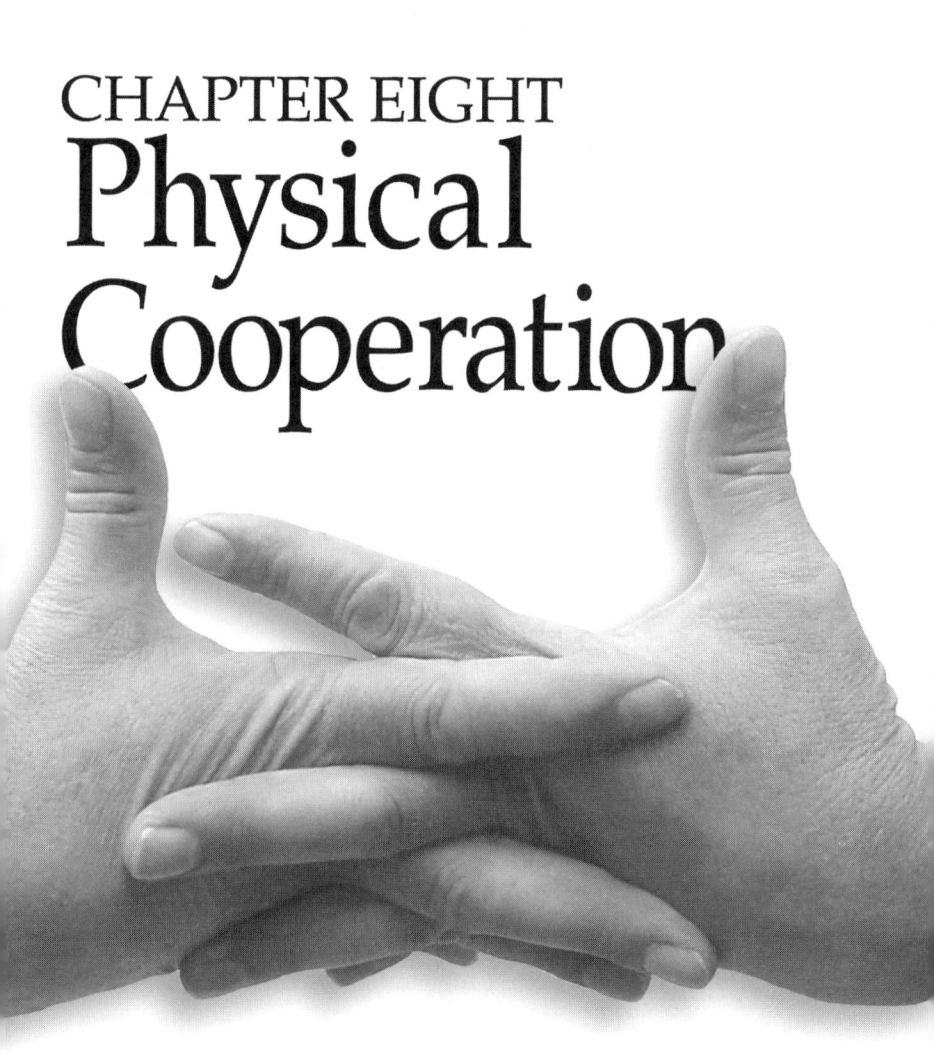

CHAPTER EIGHT
Physical Cooperation

A legitimate question.
So now we've outlined our "qualitative approach" to sport, and you might be led to ask - what about physical training? How is it effected by this perspective?

🍎 Holistic Training 🍎

An integral approach.
It should be clear that a qualitative, ethical approach doesn't negate the value or the validity of physical and technical training. It simply stresses the need to integrate the subtler aspects of human nature into the regimen. This integration serves to multiply the meaningfulness and the benefits - technical, psychological and social - of any training program.

Another notable cliché.
It's a cliché among coaches that one hour of quality work is better than two hours of sloppy or disinterested work. This should give us pause! What's being acknowledged here is that the qualities we bring to the court have a dramatic effect on the efficiency and productiveness of our physical endeavors. By placing emphasis on enthusiasm, serenity, concentration, patience and fearlessness, coaches and players can double, if not triple or quadruple, the positive effects of their physical efforts.

Personal testimony.
The amazing effects of a qualitative approach as it relates to physical proficiency has been a part of my own experience. Several people have noticed that my game doesn't suffer very much when I haven't been playing a lot of tennis. This causes bewilderment. I'm quite certain these same people resolve the anomaly in their minds (strangely, they never ask how I do it!) by

thinking of me as one who is "talented," or "naturally athletic," but this simply isn't true. Many people are far more talented than I, in the technical sense. The real solution to the puzzle lies primarily in the definition of the word "training." Training, for me, is incessant, because it's focused largely on the qualities of the player, rather than the playing, and you don't need a tennis court to enhance your serenity, or patience. So, even when I haven't been playing, I have been training, and the relationship between qualities and "performance" is so close that an improvement in the one is an improvement in the other. True, play will suffer if a degree of physical endurance isn't maintained, and, after a long lay-off, it takes a few practice sessions to hone the tennis-specific timing and sense of movement around the court, but, nevertheless, the qualitative aspect deserves the lion's share of the credit.

Bodily Wonders

Gallwey's insight. The great insight of W. Timothy Gallwey, author of "The Inner Game of Tennis," was that he recognized the inherent intelligence of the bodily nature. Many athletes try to impose motoric patterns on their bodies, without realizing that people didn't create biomechanics, nature did. Athletic actions obey the laws of motion and balance - they are learned motoric patterns that act within the confines of biomechanical laws, and the body obeys these laws, by nature. Hence, in teaching and learning physical skills, we must emphasize that we obey the body, even as we train it. Athletic actions, therefore, should feel natural, not forced or imposed. Yes, the body prefers gracefulness – that is, balance, order and harmony - above all other options!

Memory.

The body is a great store-house of memory; it forgets nothing - like a photo-plate, it captures and records everything in its environment, including its own motions. This is the much-vaunted "muscle memory" of modern parlance, and it explains why it's so important to facilitate proper technique in the early stages of training. If, through our play, we convey the message that a specific motion is suited to a specific athletic action, the body will unquestioningly integrate this set of actions into its repertoire of intelligent, adaptive faculties. Eventually, when the integration is complete, the response will be automatic, but if the programming is false, ineffectiveness and injury will result.

Avoiding trouble.

As a young child, I was largely self-taught. The technique with which I emerged from these early years was quite good, except that I used a forehand grip on the serve - I freely admit that the use of the backhand grip on the serve is one thing that doesn't seem natural in the beginning! Later, when I needed to develop a topspin delivery, which requires a continental or backhand grip, a painstaking process of re-programming and re-training was required. Hence, I say again, lay good foundations - it'll save you a lot of trouble in the future!

🍎 Learning and Teaching 🍎

Remembering versus learning.

One of the most difficult things to establish when teaching and learning strokes is the role of conscious, analytical thought. Many people say, "when I try to remember everything I'm supposed to do, the result is disastrous." This is practically inevitable. What's happened here is that learning and remembering have been

NOBLE TENNIS
THE WISDOM OF SPORT

confused. Trying to remember everything that's involved in hitting a shot, while you hit it, is like trying to force yourself to digest! It's unnatural, unnecessary, and quite absurd! Learning, on the other hand, involves watching, observing, understanding, adjusting, adapting. It's a whole different world. In remembering, we try to impose a theory on to the reality that is every moment, every action. In learning, we engage the game, thereby entering its rhythms and lessons; we come into harmony with the environment. In this, there is great joy. Perfect learning is both calm and dynamic. It's very exciting - everything is so informative! - but there is no speculation and no fear. Playing through memory is an effort of will and ambition. It negates flow and spontaneity. Learning, on the other hand, is an intelligent, joyous, serenely enthusiastic endeavor.

Try This!

Create an atmosphere of incessant learning. Address the attitude or mind-set that is appropriate to physical training, thereby avoiding a lot of frustration and failure. Ask questions of your students and ensure that they have learned not just what to do, but how to do it, why they do it, why it works, why it makes sense, etc. There is a trinity of learning, practicing and observing. This is much better than the rival trinity of being told, remembering, and drilling.

Foundations of learning.

Memory usually involves authority - we accept the word of an expert, and then try to apply their knowledge to ourselves. But in learning we are our own authority. This is absolutely necessary, because the knowledge of the coach can never produce a great athlete. Athletic competence is obtained through learning, whose fundamental prerequisite is concentrated, unbiased watching. The coach is useful because they indicate what to watch for, and they provide scenarios ("drills") that facilitate this watching. Remember, the fundamental feature of the zone is enhanced perceptiveness, but this just means we learn better in the zone, because we've given up artificial knowledge, based on memory.

Try This!

Replace "drills we are going to do" with "things we are going to learn," or "things we are going to practice."

The analytic approach.

If we insist on the techniques of memory, then, as Tennis Canada rightly says, we must literally go one step at a time. The coach and player must agree on a "teaching point," or a single element within the stroke or situation, and then focus strictly on that one thing. Thus, for instance, we can emphasize the need for a full follow-through. The key is to gauge success strictly on the basis of that single point. This will often require that we disregard, for a time at least, whether the ball goes in or out, since the follow-through is only one element amongst many. Convincing players to think this way is extremely difficult. Nevertheless, this approach can be beneficial, when working with a certain temperament, and especially when there's only one or two clearly defined elements that require attention. The "analytic approach," as I call it, is like putting a jig-saw puzzle together, but it can often seem like the puzzle is just too big, and we begin to wonder if their isn't a more natural way to get things done. This dissatisfaction impels us towards a search for holistic methods, and this is wholly good.

Using imagery.

When teaching, broad images and actual demonstrations are often preferable to detailed analysis and prescription. Thus, for example, the tennis serve can be compared to a tidal wave. In the beginning, it doesn't look like anything special - it's just slowly building momentum. Then the wave rises. This is crucial, since it must reach its peak height if it's going to produce maximum power. When it does reach its peak, it crashes down, bringing its full weight to bear. Such metaphoric images convey the *quality* of a shot, especially when the coach embodies the qualities in their demonstration, and indicates technical keys, but it leaps over many details which often serve only to produce "paralysis of analysis."

Try This!

Keep a log of useful images and metaphors that apply to different strokes or situations. This log could also include a listing of the qualitative aspects of various physical/technical elements.

The qualitative flavor.

When distinctly technical elements are introduced, they can still be placed in a qualitative context. Thus, to stick with our example of the serve, I always suggest that its keynotes are rhythm and balance. These words convey a qualitative flavor. Rhythm is synonymous with the motion, and balance is dictated mainly by the accuracy of the toss. As we continue with our exploration of the serve, I re-enforce these broad themes, placing everything within their context. Rhythm and balance are effective points of emphasis, because they are as much feelings as they are technical actions, and people can flow with a feeling, while they often stagnate with a concept.

Rhythm, rhythm, rhythm!

I have mentioned the importance of rhythm. I really don't think it can be under-estimated. The feeling for rhythmic movement is indispensable. From within the sphere of rhythm, observations and refinements can easily be made. This involves, essentially, the elements of timing, balance and coordination. Where rhythm is lacking, efficiency and effectiveness cannot emerge. Rhythm keeps us light and supple, keenly alert and able to respond to the changes in tempo and direction which, in tennis, are occurring with every ball we receive. Sport is a form of dance.

Lack of rhythm is also the source of frustration, in many cases. Very often, players say they are angry because they're making errors, but this is to mistake the effect for the cause. When we are in the zone our errors evoke observation and refinement, learning, not irritation. No, it's the feeling of being clumsy and heavy that's really upsetting. Thus, we must address the rhythm, knowing that the rest will follow. This can't be done by force; we can't force ourselves to be rhythmic, any more than we can force ourselves to go to sleep, or write a good poem. But we can eliminate those elements that negate or destroy rhythm. These are largely psychological, and are amply addressed by the whole qualitative approach. They are also physical, involving factors such as endurance, suppleness and even patterns of sleep. Indeed, for those who love summaries, we could say that the aim of the qualitative approach is to release, enhance and maintain rhythm.

NOBLE TENNIS
THE WISDOM OF SPORT

From within rhythm, which is as much a general feeling as anything else, the natural intelligence of body and mind are unimpeded. Thus, the themes of all training are rhythm, balance, timing and coordination, but the greatest, the first amongst these, is rhythm.

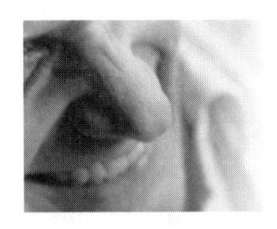

Try This!

Incorporate rhythm as a central theme at all levels of playing and teaching. Explain, for instance, that the primary purpose of the warm-up is to establish a light or slow rhythm, which can then be increased. Address rhythm whenever necessary, before launching into a million technical observations. Do exercises whose theme is the ability to respond to or create different tempos, and include rhythmic exercises, perhaps even dance lessons, as part of off-court training. Play music when playing (I've found a Strauss waltz can be quite effective), and always remember: sport is a form of dance.

Swing Freely!

When playing or teaching at any level, the most crucial thing is a commitment to "swing freely." This is an attitude and applies to all sports, whether they involve actual "swinging" or not. Maintain a happy rhythm, stay supple, free, responsive. From within that space, refinements can be made. Thus, with beginning tennis players, let them start by just swinging at the ball. Who knows, a lot may happen naturally, without interference. In the beginning, the work of the coach may just be to encourage and facilitate this feeling, to help people to feel comfortable enough that they'll let themselves go, and let themselves flow. Then you'll see what you have to work with, and you can take steps that are appropriate to the particular person, as opposed to a theoretical textbook. I think you'll find that this approach is a lot more fun for everyone than the studied, heavy, technical approach which states that everyone must impose a theory on to the natural intelligence and rhythm which is who and what they are.

🍎 Nutrition and Fitness 🍎

Dietary advice.

As regards diet, the best themes are balance and common sense. In an age where everyone and their pet canary has a theory about what's good for you and what isn't, what leads to "peak performance" and what doesn't, what causes disease and what doesn't, the best thing is to stand above this fray (whose hidden theme is often the search for personal profit), and simply use your own mind, aided by some rudimentary knowledge. This knowledge should include qualitative and psychological elements. For example: it is best if we can enjoy and appreciate the food we eat; we shouldn't eat too quickly, and we should avoid eating "on the fly." An attitude of appreciation and care for the speed of consumption will greatly aid the processes of digestion, and will reflect qualities, such as patience, which are always beneficial, and which can be incessantly cultivated. Above all, we must take the link between the physical and the psychic more seriously. Indeed, most people could do more for their health by eliminating depression, anxiety and scattered thinking, than by counting the calories in their frozen dinner!

NOBLE ⊙ TENNIS
THE WISDOM OF SPORT

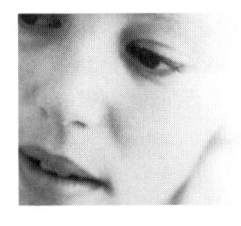

Try This!

As you observe the barrage of technological advances in the realm of physical training and nutrition, ask yourself what is necessary, what is essential, and what is not. Are you being sucked into a preoccupation with things that don't really effect the ultimate purpose of sport – the growth and development of human beings, as human beings, and the attainment of the creative zone?

Exceptional examples.

Also, it should be realized that diet is highly individual. Lorne Main was the world tennis champion in the men's over 55 category when I was training at All-Canadian. He could rally from the baseline forever, and was known for his superabundance of energy. Now, in my three years at the Academy I spent a lot of time with Lorne - we even lived in the same house one year - but, apart from one fork-full of lasagna, the only things I ever saw him eat were "mars" chocolate bars, which he preferred frozen, "blizzards" from Dairy Queen, diet Coke and Tim Horton's coffee! I kid you not. Or, here's another exceptional and strange case: at one of the facilities where I train, I find I suffer from spells of dizziness and loss of energy. In combating this condition I've tried many things, but only one has worked, and that's the consumption of a chocolate bar at the moment the symptoms arise. Within fifteen minutes of eating the chocolate my energy levels return to normal, and stay that way. Now I'm not suggesting that athletes should turn to "junk-food" diets, but I am noting that flexibility and an individualized approach must exist side-by-side with the general principles of healthy dietary habits. We mustn't be fanatical or dogmatic. People should observe the response of their bodies to various foods and environments, and adjust accordingly (note: even the Dalai Lama - the spiritual and political leader of Tibetan Buddhism - had to give up his vegetarian diet, when it made him ill).

Simple methods.

When it comes to off-court physical training, the principles of simplicity, common sense and individualization should again apply. I've found that simple regimens which combine things like running and biking, push-ups and crunches (previously known as sit-ups), yogic stretching, on-court agility exercises, wind-sprints and wall-sits - none of which requires advanced technology, huge outlays of money, or, indeed, anything beyond our own body weight (except for the bike) - are quite sufficient to maintain a high degree of physical fitness.

Fitness as an effect.

It's extremely beneficial if physical exercise coincides with useful activity. For instance, one winter I worked with a friend who was in "forest management." This involved trudging through knee-high snow, often in minus twenty degree weather, cutting down giant trees with a heavy chainsaw, trimming the trees, cutting them into logs, hauling them on to a snowmobile, cutting the logs into pieces, splitting the pieces with an axe, throwing the wood into a pick-up truck, delivering and unloading it, and, in some cases, stacking the wood into large, orderly rows! In the process of doing this work, I learned an enormous amount about different trees - their names, properties, etc., I helped people in my community who needed firewood, I breathed fresh air and got "close to nature," I became oblivious to relative extremes of cold and fatigue, thereby building character and confidence while overcoming the modern obsession with comfort and luxury, I earned a bit of money, and, *incidentally*, I've never been stronger in my life! I think this kind of endeavor is much healthier than the fitness craze of the late twentieth century. Modern fitness clubs are usually elitist and cloistered, and the endeavors of its members are all-too-often driven by vanity and paranoia. "Fitness" is best understood when it applies to the whole person, not just their tissues and fibres!

Try This!

Try to arrange for physical fitness to emerge as an effect of useful activity. If this seems impossible, try at least to do fitness in beautiful, outdoor, natural settings.

Enthusiasm and endurance.

Finally, on the topic of physical fitness, it needs to be noted that the degree of endurance is greatly effected by the degree of enthusiasm. I've experienced days when I seem to lack endurance, even though I've been working out regularly; and, conversely, there are times when I feel I could go on and on, even though I haven't been working out "in the gym." Thus, physical fitness is certainly necessary, but we must never forget the ever-present influence of the qualitative dimension.

"Yoga."

Depth and quality can always be introduced into physical actions. Take, for example, stretching. Most players are negligent when it comes to preparing their body for the rigors of sport. As a junior, I was constantly told to stretch before I played, but it seemed so boring, so trivial. Stretching doesn't mean anything, so it's not interesting. However, if we combine physical stretches with an emphasis on serenity, aided by rhythmic breathing and graceful transitions between stretches, then we've suddenly arrived at what is popularly called yoga. In India, these yogic exercises have been practiced for centuries, with a full understanding of their psychological significance. As a result of this yogic approach to stretching, the empty, forceful, preliminary movements of the body are transformed into meaningful gestures, which prepare the entire person for play. I've introduced yogic sequences to players as young as ten years old, with good results. Surely, depth is preferable to shallowness.

Try This!

Replace "stretching" with "yoga," recalling that suppleness and rhythm are the prerequisites of athletic greatness.

🍎 The Bigger Picture 🍎

The qualitative fabric of life.

It's useful to reflect that people spend up to 50% of their lives eating, sleeping and grooming. This is quite natural, and maybe even necessary. The problem is that such "mundane" activities are usually separated from the qualities that require development. Indeed, most people lack the indispensable qualities precisely because they treat physical activities in a purely mechanical way, rather than seeing them as opportunities for qualitative growth. Serenity and enthusiasm can't be fully and properly developed if we only take them seriously during the few hours we spend on the tennis court! No, they must be woven into the fabric of our daily lives, and life, as a whole, must become a qualitative investigation, a qualitative endeavor. This may seem burdensome and onerous to some, but, to those who are ready, it will hold out the prospect of sustained joy, achieved through the qualitative transformation of life. Just imagine - every moment a pathway to the nobility and happiness of the zone. Now that's something worth striving for! Remember, wisdom is the unification and harmonization of things that seem separate, and one of the highest forms of wisdom is the unification of the physical and psychological, or the quantitative and the qualitative, aspects of existence.

Try This!

Seek always to discover and import aspects of quality and meaning into physical training. The infusion of quality into the realm of quantity is our central task.

The joy of learning.

In concluding, I'd like to emphasize the great joy of technical improvement, physical proficiency and tactical wherewithal. I've been playing tennis for a long time, and yet scarcely a week goes by when I don't achieve some new insight of a technical, biomechanical, physical or strategical (i.e. geometrical) nature. Indeed, my playing and teaching has continually improved as a result of constant learning. Tennis, it seems, contains an infinity of possibilities, and it's truly exhilarating - fun - to explore its fathomless depths. However, tennis, like all sports, has a deeper and wider significance than is contained in its strokes and strategies. The young person that you train might be a future leader, or a future tyrant. Which of these outcomes do your methods support? The great coach will emphasize and radiate his or her principles, and these will saturate all their work and relationships. Even as they teach physical skills, they will never forget the ultimate importance of 'the intangibles'; they will never regard physical and technical prowess as an end-in-itself, but will always see it as a means to a nobler end. Sport and nobility - the two should be inseparable.

NOBLE TENNIS
THE WISDOM OF SPORT

CHAPTER NINE
Odds & Ends

Filling in the blanks.

The wisdom of sport produces a change of perspective concerning the whys and the wherefores, the meaning and purpose, of the athletic enterprise. From this new perspective, everything looks different; everything dies and is reborn in a new shape, a shape that is less violent and shallow than before. In this chapter, I look at how the wisdom of sport and the qualitative approach changes our perception of some common aspects and ideas about sport.

🍎 Sport: A Non-Violent Sphere 🍎

A different view of competition.

How does a philosophy of perfectment and an ethos of harmony think and feel about competitions? A competition is a structured opportunity to discover where mastery has been attained and where it is lacking. Thus, it is the duty of the contestants to reveal weaknesses and demonstrate strengths. This perspective, when really grasped, changes the whole complexion of the event. It purifies the notion of "strategy and tactics," and it engenders feelings of respect and camaraderie between and amongst the contestants. It's an understanding that is reflected, I think, in the way athletes bow to each other in the martial arts tradition. It eliminates the feelings of hostility and fear that seem to permeate the competitive atmosphere.

Ending malice.

The violence of strategy and tactics begins when they're seen as ways of defeating an opponent, whom we regard as the enemy. When they are seen as elements of perfectment, the malice associated with them disappears, just as it disappears from "competition."

Try This!

See if you can eliminate all traces of aggression and hostility from the way you speak about sport in its psychological, physical, tactical and technical aspects. This will be a natural tendency when you change your thoughts about the game, and the spirit behind words is more important than the words themselves, but finding new terminology takes some conscious effort. For instance, I have replaced the idea of a "forcing" shot with that of a "building" shot. Eventually, I hope to arrive at a whole new vocabulary for tennis, based on harmony as the keynote. All contributions to this task will be greatly appreciated.

Decision-making and the zone.

In the zone, harmonization and intelligence manifest spontaneously and intuitively. This heightened perceptiveness and responsiveness is joy. Hence, in the zone, there's no "decision-making," as normally understood. The need to make a decision implies uncertainty, confusion. This does not exist in the zone. Instead, there is spontaneous harmonization and active intelligence, coupled with sensitive observation and a feeling of lightness that borders on flight. Where there is clarity, there is no "choice." Therefore, strive for clarity. This is achieved when players understand their sport, when they are free from fear and doubt, and when they know and have trained the basic, foundational patterns that coincide with their position or game-style. In this latter connection, I recommend that coaches train very realistic or game-like patterns, as opposed to isolated techniques or skills. Work with students so that they understand the most intelligent response in various situations, and then ensure that they have the skills to implement those responses. In the words of Tennis Canada – we should know *what* we are doing, before we address *how* we do it. It is a great liberation when the chaos of "choice" is replaced by the simplicity of clarity, which comes with understanding and training.

Gamesmanship.

In all honesty, this word can be translated as *cruelty*. Gamesmanship is aggressive and antagonistic strategy; it is the destructive use of psychology - an attempt to weaken or degrade a person at mental and emotional levels. The user of gamesmanship seeks to instill distraction and/or doubt and/or fear in another human being. This requires that we see other people as enemies, and this, in turn, is a crime against human dignity and development; it cannot be countenanced. The ideas and attitudes that produce gamesmanship are identical to those that produce cruelty and warfare in any and every context. Need I say more?

Unpleasant but useful times.

As a junior I was extremely vulnerable to gamesmanship, especially when employed by people who were my friends in off-court settings, but who were temporarily transformed by the competitive notion that all men are enemies once they enter a sports arena! The use of intimidation and cruelty was horrible to me, and I shrank in its presence - the perfect victim. If someone said, "this guy is so bad!" I would listen, thereby allowing the suggestion to cause distraction and doubt.

Later, when I was coming into my own, so to speak, I faced an ultimate test of gamesmanship. It was in the quarter-finals of an open event, and I was playing against a man who epitomized gamesmanship in all its forms. Already, this obnoxious creature had defeated the second seed, largely by the use of his abusive and distracting methods. The tournament director was also intimidated, or perhaps even amused, for he would not employ the code of conduct against the perpetrator, so I knew I was on my own; I knew I would have to demonstrate a perfect degree of fearlessness and composure; I knew that the qualities, not the antics, would have to be the decisive factor. In this endeavor I succeeded, and I won the match 6-4, 7-5. This was a major milestone for me, and could perhaps be cited as the moment when I definitely realized that I had something to say about the power of qualitative training.

I relate this story because it illustrates that while qualitative coaches and players will always eschew every form of gamesmanship, and while tournament referees must be increasingly encouraged to enforce codes of conduct, the perpetrators of gamesmanship will always be with us, and a proper attitude towards such encounters must be cultivated. The man against whom I played was an opportunity. That's the only way to see it. He provided a chance to test and demonstrate the efficacy of the inner strength – the serenity, concentration, patience and fearlessness – I had developed. This, then, was a victory over all gamesmanship - a demonstration that there's something better and more effectual than cruelty and manipulation. Truly, people like the man I played are doing no good for themselves, and they should not feel it's their prerogative to attempt the psychic damaging of others. Nevertheless, such people are out there, and they do serve a purpose.

Ethics and the zone.

Unethical, destructive behavior does not exist in the zone. In 1985, I went to the U.S. Open and saw John Mcenroe, the prototypical athletic miscreant, play a match in the zone. It was the quarter-finals, and he defeated Joakim Nystrom of Sweden, then ranked around #10 in the world, 6-1, 6-0, 7-5. Mcenroe was brilliant, even masterful. He radiated a sense of total calmness and composure; he demonstrated perfect anticipation and responsiveness, suppleness, power, control. The match lasted for at least two hours, and Mcenroe didn't utter a single word. Even in the third set, when Nystrom made things close, Mcenroe was the very picture of propriety.

Thus, while "good behavior" isn't a definition of the zone, it is one of its distinguishing features. This makes perfect sense, since all destructive behavior is based on propensities within the psyche. A person who is in the zone consists of a psychological state that is composed of enthusiasm, serenity, patience, concentration and fearlessness, and these, by their nature, exclude destructiveness, anger and violence. Hence, no matter what the external situation the person who is in the zone will not recognize behaviors that we rightly call "unethical" as live possibilities; it won't even cross their mind. The zone, therefore, is the *solution* to misbehavior.

Sincerity.

The qualitative approach puts the heart back into sport. Under its influence sportsmanship becomes a sincere expression of where a person's coming from, not just a pretencious behavioral display. Yes, it's possible to say "have a good match," and actually mean it! Today, people make jokes about the natural insincerity of such comments. For example, when a tennis ball hits the tape and dribbles over the sportsman expresses regret at winning a point by luck, but today if a person says "sorry," the other will often say "no you're not," and laugh, as if such a sentiment were beyond the reach of human feeling! They don't realize that such jests reveal the full degeneracy of sport. Indeed, the need is very dire when even the most rudimentary goodwill is considered beyond the scope of human nature.

Try This!

Revive in yourself and in your students/ children the ideal of the honorable sportsman, the noble amateur. This is a worthy ideal, one that allows for the development of potential without the ugliness that surrounds athletics today. Speak of these things; teach the rules of sportsmanship and applaud their expression; create scenarios to practice responding with dignity and intelligence – and sometimes with indignation – to improper conduct. Make it real!

"Sport psychology," "Sport Science," and Other Red Herrings

Psychology.

Modern, behavioral psychology is an extraordinarily shallow approach to "the science of the soul" (psyche is derived from Greek, and means soul). Even its use of the phrase "peak performance" betrays its lack of depth, since a performance is an act, and an actor is one who pretends to be something they are not. The athlete who focuses on performance need not address the question of *who they are*; instead, they simply adapt *what they do* to the requirements of an immediate, material objective.

Under this system the person fails to really change and grow, even if they're winning everything in sight. This shallowness of approach explains how athletes can be so magnificent on the court or field, and so uncouth, immoral, uncontrolled, immature and incompetent when outside the playing area. Behavioral psychology fragments life into various tasks and performances, while disallowing the inner development that produces integral human beings, beings who are competent at life - at being human - rather than simply at "tasks," like a computer. When this fragmentary approach rules, the sense of synthesis is lost: one's athletic enterprise has no connection to one's life, seen as a whole, or to one's community, society, or the world at large. Sport, in this case, becomes irrelevant to the greater good, at best, and, at worst, it becomes a positive detriment.

The props of shallowness.

The shallowness of sport is aided by technology, because it promotes brute force as the fundamental aspect of sport. Further, it places all our focus on external appendages to the athlete, rather than internal resources. All technology is meant to compensate for human limitations, but are we really as limited as we think? Shallowness is also promoted by commercialism. Great athletes are seen as commodities, rather than as humans. Who benefits when people tramp all over the world, seeing nothing but airplanes, hotel rooms and tennis courts? The time has come to put humans first.

Try This!

If you travel with athletes, be it to a nearby city or around the world, insist that the travel include elements of cultural discovery and educational enlargement.

Always, always stress and reveal the bigger picture. This will improve inward and outward health, as well as athletic "performance."

Dangers of "goal-setting."

Today, goal-setting is proclaimed to the skies, but it isn't so straightforwardly wonderful. Material or outcome-oriented goals always produce fear - of failure, humiliation, etc., and this sets the stage for: a) cheating, in its many forms, including the use of illegal and damaging drugs; b) a hostile, cruel and joyless competitiveness; c) injuries, caused by over-training, coupled with the tension of fear; and d) an inability to rise to the zone, whose chief requirements are fearlessness and a serenely enthusiastic absorption in "the now." Further, it should be noted that when a person sets a material goal, they prescribe a limit. People try to decide what they will or will not, can or cannot achieve, but this is both unhealthy and unwise. Such thinking usually negates openness to the flow of life, which may lead us in many and varied directions, while also arbitrarily circumscribing a potential that could be much greater than we imagine. Goal-setting, in other words, is capable of producing a closed, narrow and selfish mind, which, driven by fear, pursues its ends in a violent and irrational manner.

A cautious deployment.

Nevertheless, goal-setting can be very useful, if it's done with fearlessness, and if it doesn't close our minds to unforeseen possibilities and circumstances. If goal-setting is to operate in this way, certain things should be recognized, as follows: a) goal-setting should focus on the attainment of capacities, not on speculation about the results these capacities will bring about. In particular, the cultivation of the indispensable qualities should be stressed, as well as the attainment of physical, tactical and technical abilities. After this, we must simply *let* the results flow; b) the main value of a goal-setting program, rigorously adhered to, is that it produces discipline and intensity, plus an ability for self-observation and self-knowledge. Coaches should keep this in mind, and should realize that while the adolescent is preoccupied with the foreground, with immediate results, the mature coach has a view of the bigger picture, and the long-term effects of the training they initiate; and c) in the normal development of a human being, the setting of selfish and/or self-centered goals is only a phase, and, as they mature, the need for such activity will lessen. Increasingly, the person will be so qualitative in their thinking, and so open to the flow of life, that they will live entirely in the zone - i.e. without personally formulated goals of any kind, but with total fearlessness and enthusiasm, and with great perceptiveness and responsiveness.

A call to discrimination.

Given the ambiguous stature of goal-setting, it becomes clear that the coach must demonstrate discrimination. If a player is resisting a goal-setting program, is it because they're lazy, or is it because they've outgrown it? And, conversely, if they embrace goal-setting, is it due to fear and violent ambition, or is it because they have a thirst for self-knowledge and striving? These things make a big difference! After all, there's nothing *inherently* good about goal-setting. All the worst tyrants in history have been very focused, very "goal-oriented" people. Thus, it's not so much the goal, but who sets it, and why, that really counts.

Try This!

If you elect to do a goal-setting program, I recommend a three-tiered system. You will need three sheets of paper. On the first sheet are listed the goals. On the second sheet are listed the qualitative and quantitative aspects that are relevant to the meeting of the goal. These should be quite specific, for they will be assessed each day with a mark out of ten, based on the extent to which that quality or activity was carried through. The third sheet is a graph which lists the days of the month on the top and the numbered qualities and/or activities on sheet number two. It is here that marks are recorded. As a youngster, I found this organization helpful and efficient.

"Just say no."

While we're on the topic of discrimination, I should raise another pertinent issue - knowing when *not* to coach. Coaches will sometimes run into players (and parents) who refuse any qualitative development, and who use tennis as an outlet for positively harmful and destructive energies. In such cases, a refusal to participate may be the most harmless thing, though the coach should discriminate carefully, recognizing when the misdirected energies are the result of removable fears, etc. Quite often, people at this extreme edge of materialism and fear are talented in the technical and physical sense, and the temptation to work with them can be quite strong. In this case, the coach must address their motives. The person who has overcome egoistic ambition will always do the right thing, and the best coach in the world may or may not have a national champion under her wing. They won't mind either way. We must remember that the measure of success under the qualitative approach is very different, and we can't expect others to mature if the leaders aren't leading.

An important lesson.
Once, a teacher handed his student a copy of the *I Ching* (a Chinese text, meaning "Book of Changes"), and suggested that through its study a great realization would be made. With this in mind, the student read the book aloud, from cover to cover. When this was done, the teacher asked if the student had got the point. The student said "no," and the teacher suggested that the book be read again. When it was done, the teacher asked the student if they had got the point. The student said "no," and began again. Half way through the third consecutive reading, the teacher raised his hand and said the lesson was over - the realization had been made. The student was utterly bewildered, and asked what the point had been. The teacher smiled and said, "discipline." In this way, the teacher demonstrated the real value of setting a goal.

Emotion.
Today, emotion is highly touted. Indeed, next to physical health and comfort, nothing is so absorbing to the average person as their moods. And yet, there is absolutely no emotion in the zone, and I affirm that all emotion is surpassed as the human psyche matures. Emotion is limiting, and inherently neurotic. But don't jump to the wrong conclusion - I am not advocating the absence of feelings, aspirations, or even desires. We must be very specific here, and get things really clear. The sensitive, feeling aspect of human nature is a great and wondrous garden, but emotion is like a weed that smothers the better, more beautiful plants.

Emotion, happiness and joy.
An emotion is a personal reaction to a set of stimuli, based on fear, possessiveness, selfishness and ignorance. These things, in turn, tend to produce chaos, disharmony and ugliness, all of which

are contrary to the noble and the beautiful. Contrary to popular belief, joy is not an emotion, nor is happiness. Happiness is the feeling we have in the zone, and the zone is a place where the sense of separative, insecure individuality has disappeared. It is a place where the preconditions of emotion do not exist. When the zone is stabilized through understanding and training, happiness merges into joy, which is a more permanent state. Notice, again, how emotion requires that the sense of separative individuality be completely or partially ascendant. This separative self is invariably afraid - it feels itself alone in a hostile environment, and seeks control, possessions, security, pleasures, etc. When these are lost, or not obtained in the first place, the little self becomes very angry and/or sad. Emotion, therefore, which is the chief characteristic of the small, isolated ego, is contrary to the zone, and, hence, to both happiness and joy.

Pleasure and Pain.

The person who lives in the emotions can feel pleasure and pain, but pleasure is fleeting and pain is ubiquitous, it is everywhere, so the emotional person is constantly threatened by anger and/or desperation and/or depression. Both pleasure and pain are forms of irritation, and that's why all emotional people are essentially irritable, unstable, moody, irrational and unclear. The chaos, cruelty, absurdity and suffering of the world is largely the result of uncontrolled, falsely glorified emotion. Thus, in striving to the zone, we should encourage ourselves and others to demonstrate steadfastness of aspiration, and not to be the victim of moods, or fleeting external conditions.

🍎 Final Aces 🍎

Master-class program.

In the past two years, I've introduced what I call the "master class program" to several students. The idea was inspired by the film "Searching for Bobby Fisher," in which the coach awards the student a certificate, saying that he's an accomplished or masterful chess player. I took this idea and expanded it, until it became a comprehensive training regimen. The program consists, so far, of six degrees. Each degree contains ten levels, every level focusing on a skill and/or quality. In the course of weekly lessons, players can earn "master class points" as they do exercises that emphasize the stated theme of the level. To complete a level, the student must earn fifty points, and then pass a test in which their competency in the specified area is affirmed. Each player keeps a log, in which they record what degree and level they are at, and how many points they've earned. For every level attained, I award a star or sticker, and with every degree - a certificate. This course has many benefits, including its ability to keep players focused on mastering the game, rather than external results. The themes cycle through all the major strokes and situations, with increasing refinement and exactitude being expected at every turn of the spiral, so to speak. Also, every degree has an over-arching theme. Degree one, for instance, emphasizes "enthusiasm and perseverance," while in degree six the player has arrived at the possibility of "training in the zone." The training, of course, becomes increasingly focused on the inner aspects, as the technical skills are stabilized. In degree six, for example, level I focuses on "stability," achieved mainly through silence. Thus, the master class program leads the student towards the true, lasting issues and benefits of athletic training.

A new cliche.

When the qualitative approach takes hold, everything becomes fresh and new. It breeds a new language, and even new cliches. Thus, for instance, we used to say "it's not if you win or lose, it's how you play the game." This, by discouraging rampant, mindless competitiveness, serves a definite purpose, and there are many people who could still learn a lot from this phrase. However, it doesn't meet the needs of the person who's ready for the qualitative approach - the person who's *beyond* competition for it's own sake, and who needs a why for the game, not just a how. Thus, I offer the following: it's not how you play the game, it's who plays it.

The Savory Solution.

It is wonderful if people can savor what they do and experience. To savor is to take delight in something, like a wonderful meal whose every morsel is something special, something we would never rush, and something we do just for itself, not for a reward beyond the doing. The great meal is its own reward. What things do you savor? The idea of savoring tennis encompasses and affirms many of the noble qualities we've discussed in this book. Savoring affirms enthusiasm for the thing being savored; it produces serenity, for there is nowhere else in the world we'd rather be and nothing we'd rather be doing; it generates concentration – like a kid staring at the lollypop as he licks and sucks; and it makes us patient, for we want to enjoy every moment of the process. Unfortunately, most people never experience pure savoring. This is because even as they enjoy something, they are afraid - afraid that they will never have it again, or that it might be bad for them, or that it costs too much, or some other such thing. Thus, only the fearless person, the person who is free from the speculations and greediness of the little ego, can truly savor, truly take delight in any wonderful thing. Our task, then, is to be *able* to savor sport as the wonderful thing it is.

A delightful method.

For many years, I have experienced the problem of the wandering mind. Typically, I am strong at the beginning of a tennis match, but weak in the middle. This is so because my mind shoots ahead to the end of the match. This demonstrates an over-abundance of analytic thought, which always wants to see how things will or could turn out. The busy mind, the mind that always wants to know "the bottom line," how to get from A to B in the shortest way, is babbling! This shooting off to the future is also tinged with the egoism that wants to talk about what happened, and to speculate on what might happen. The typical response to this state of affairs is to demand concentration, but I have found that to affirm savoring is far more effective. When I affirm that I am too busy savoring the tennis to speculate over it, there is a tactile element of attraction, and this makes concentration simple and natural. This is similar to when people say that they wish to enjoy themselves, but whereas enjoyment is somewhat abstract, savoring is quite concrete. When the attitude of savoring is free from fear, when you savor without a future reward or failure in mind, then you are in the best possible frame of mind. Try it, and see for yourself.

NOBLE TENNIS
THE WISDOM OF SPORT

Nobility.

I will close by citing the lyrics to a song, taken from the Alan Lerner and Frederick Lowe musical production, "Camelot." It's sung by Sir Lancelot, as he prepares to go to Camelot and join the knights of the round table. Perhaps here we have a goal for the person who embraces the thought of noble tennis:

> The soul of a knight should be a thing remarkable,
> his heart and his mind as pure as morning dew;
> with the will and the self-restraint
> that's the envy of every saint,
> he could easily work a miracle or two...
>
> But where in the world
> Is there in the world
> A man so extraordinaire?
>
> C'est moi! C'est moi!
> I blush to disclose,
> I'm much too noble to lie,
> that man in whom these qualities bloom,
> c'est moi, c'est moi, 'tis I.
>
> I've never strayed from all I believe,
> I'm blessed with an iron will;
> had I been made the partner of Eve,
> we'd be in Eden still!

NOBLE TENNIS
THE WISDOM OF SPORT

C'est moi! C'est moi!
The angels have chose
to fight their battles below,
and here am I, as pure as a prayer,
incredibly clean, with virtue to spare,
the godliest man I know!

C'est moi!

NOBLE TENNIS
THE WISDOM OF SPORT

CHAPTER TEN
The Wisdom of Sport

Reclaiming sport.

The wisdom of sport lies in its ability to evoke and train the finest and noblest aspects of human nature. This has been known throughout the ages, and it's only in the twentieth century that we have bastardized and belittled the athletic enterprise, even as we celebrate it like never before. The time has come to reclaim sport from shallow, shortsighted influences, and to restore its sense of meaning and purpose. That's what this book has been about.

🎾 Philosophies of Sport 🎾

Philosophy: The Fifth Column.

When I say sport has been "belittled," I mean it's lost something, and that something is philosophy. Philosophy means "the love of wisdom." It begins with the realization that specific things, like sports, are related to bigger and more universal things, like "life," or "happiness," or "society," or "the cosmos." Today, these bigger questions and concerns, these greater realities and possibilities, have been largely forgotten. We tend to regard sports as physical sciences, with the aim of efficiency in competition, but the question remains - *to what end?* What is the greater purpose of sport? Is there something to be gained through athletics, besides a great forehand, or a super jump-shot? Today, we appeal to various, mainly external things - like rankings, fame and money - and we say these justify hard work and enterprise; or we focus on the benefits of sport in terms of physical health and longevity. Material rewards, however, are fleeting - a ranking is here today and gone tomorrow, and even physical health is only a limited boon, if we have no sense of meaning and purpose in our existence. And so we're still left with the problem of whether there are any *deep and lasting* benefits of sport. To answer this question, we need philosophy.

Eastern athletics.

In India and the Far East, the traditional understanding of sports (i.e. physical disciplines, including arts and crafts) is distinctly philosophical. The task of the athlete is to cultivate those states of being and those capacities, or virtues - such as patient discipline, quiescent serenity and egoless concentration - which make them a fit vehicle for the expression of "That," or "the Tao," or "the Higher Self." In all cases, what's indicated by these terms is an intelligence, a creativeness, a perceptiveness, a sensitivity and a responsiveness that far outstrips that of the "normal," isolated, individualistic, worrying, wanting, grasping ego, or self. What is indicated, in other words, is "the zone." The zone is a place of happiness, joy, efficiency and effectiveness. In the zone, our best flows from us in a completely natural and effortless way. Through sport, we can discover that place, and stabilize ourselves within it. Thus, the zone isn't meant to be a vague experience, which happens every once and a while, for no known reason, and which is only applicable in the athletic setting. On the contrary, the idea is that the zone can become our normal or regular state of being, thereby transforming and uplifting all of life. That, to be sure, is a philosophical idea - one that relates to greater issues of life and happiness, and it provides an excellent foundation for athletic training.

Western athletics.

In the West, until recently, the aspect of philosophy called morality and ethics has been greatly emphasized. The Olympic ideal of brotherhood and goodwill is an obvious example; and, similarly, in the British school system, sport was regarded as a necessary element in the development of "character." Such character consisted largely of the social virtues, including the sense of justice and fair play, teamwork, dedication, etc. These ideas were borrowed mainly from the Ancient Greeks, who were acutely aware of the relationship between sport and philosophy. They realized that athletic discipline, apart from its inherent value as a channeler for the energies of youth, was an excellent preliminary for future endeavors and understandings of a broader, deeper, more distinctly philosophical nature. Indeed, Socrates, Plato and Pythagoras were all excellent athletes in their youths. That's noteworthy, don't you think?

The Big Picture

The fifth column.
Ultimately, these philosophical conceptions of sport are the only things that render it noble, beautiful and valuable. Indeed, as a tennis coach I can't see any legitimate justification for sport apart from its philosophical aspects. True, we can speak of sport as it relates to "culture" and "education" and "psychology," but these only find their worth and measure as they relate to a broader realization of meaning and purpose in human existence. How do we know *what* to teach if we don't know *why* we're teaching? Thus, the "global approach" to sport, which is often said to include psychological, physical, tactical and technical components, isn't truly global until it includes this final element, this fifth column – philosophy. Philosophy, apart from its ability to enhance the "performance" of an athlete, provides the athletic enterprise with a justification and a trans-personal meaning.

A harmful narcotic.
Apart from its value as a proponent of wisdom, sport is positively irresponsible. When seen within the context of world affairs, troubled as they are, how can we justify the huge expenditures of time and money that people spend in watching and playing

sports? People use sport to distract themselves, they gamble their money away, they spend hour after hour watching sports, discussing sports, playing sports, arguing over sports, studying sports. To what end? Today, sport is really an opiate of the people, and the inertia it causes - in relation to the serious yet exciting crises and opportunities of the present age - is simply deplorable. Further, sport, as represented and practiced today, is a handmaiden for almost every human vice. Violence, in its many forms - physical, emotional and mental, fanaticism, greed, consumerism, glorification of the physical at the expense of the subtle and spiritual - these are destroying the world, and sport, in many and even most cases, is an active proponent of them all. Enough! We're fiddling while Rome burns. Humanity must begin expressing its noble qualities - that's the solution to our problems and our misery, and sport, if it's going to be a worldwide force, it must be a force for good. Through sport, the virtues of human nature can be discovered, exposed, trained and stabilized. Therein lies its nobility, and its validity within a responsible and uplifting view of human affairs, human existence and human happiness.

Exciting possibilities.

The approach to sport that emphasizes noble qualities is exciting in its implications and possibilities: in the first place, it provides sport with the philosophical and social value that it sorely lacks today. But, more than this, the virtues, as we've seen, are the key to sincere and spontaneous sportsmanship, effective and efficient training - both physical and psychological, and, last but not least, the zone. Yes, the zone, that glorious but little understood experience, is inseparable from the "qualitative approach." The zone isn't merely a set of behaviors that are conducive to "peak performance." No, it's *a state of being*, and the behaviors that sport psychologists applaud and encourage are *natural* expressions of that state of being. Hence, wisdom psychology, or depth psychology, places its emphasis on inner states, achieved through the conscious expression of qualities. These qualities are actually the contents of the zone, and their cultivation is the true meaning of the term "ethics." In this way, ethical training stops being an onerous duty and becomes instead a pathway to the grace, freedom, happiness and beauty of the zone.

The forgotten ingredient.

The nobility, beauty and effectiveness of virtue, which has been heralded by religions and philosophies in all ages, is now being re-affirmed. There's something ironic in all this, don't you think? For, in the age where everyone is supposedly concerned with "success" and "efficiency" and "empowerment" and "happiness," we have shunned and/or marginalized the one thing that lets them all occur in a harmless and natural way - *virtue*. Virtue is the language and the action of wisdom. This wisdom is badly needed in the athletic realm, and in the world as a whole. Is anybody interested?

A Concluding Analogy

A Concluding Analogy

Let us compare a human being to a tree. The tree has a purpose. It's aim, or goal, is to become *fully* a tree; to express its tree-ness in the most complete way it can. In striving towards this end the tree exhibits an ability to *cooperate* with natural processes of growth. It accepts and incorporates the sun, rain and soil, which are provided by nature; it eliminates impurities, and overcomes obstacles. In this process, the tree becomes strong and healthy, and, as it does so, it begins to demonstrate its hidden powers and capacities. Think about the wondrous character of a tree: it provides the oxygen without which many forms of life could not occur; it eliminates impurities from the environment; it provides food and shelter for many different life-forms; it's a thing of inspiring beauty; it is available for purposes of human construction and creativity.

Now let's think about human beings. Couldn't we say that our task is to become fully human? Of course we could. A human being is a distinctly psychological form of life, and this means we must cooperate with our inner nature, as well as the outer. We must harmonize with the universal energies of enthusiasm and serenity, which are to the human soul what sun and rain are too the tree; we must overcome obstacles, through concentration, patience and knowledge, all of which are gained through training; and we must eliminate the impurities of fear and doubt, which sap our strength and halt the processes of growth. The results of this process are at least as grand as they were for the tree. A mature, responsible human being is a creative wonder, whose faculties and capacities may be greater than anyone has yet imagined.

NOBLE TENNIS
THE WISDOM OF SPORT

The qualities outlined in this book represent a general formula, or structure, for entering the path that leads to the growth and development of human beings. Sport, like all human institutions and endeavors, serves its truest and highest purpose when it acts as an aid in this process - like fertilizer for the tree, or yeast in dough. Humans, unlike trees, have the ability to resist their own evolution, or growth, or maturation. They do this when they accept and propagate impurities, like fear, and when they become distracted by things that bear no relation to their qualitative development. Today, this is being done all the time, in all areas of life, and the result is a withered, frustrated humanity. So let's reverse the trend - let's affirm the value of being human. Then, the stalk of the indispensable qualities will yield the flower of nobility, and the earth will be immeasurably enriched.

NOBLE TENNIS
THE WISDOM OF SPORT

NOBLE TENNIS
THE WISDOM OF SPORT

Appendices

🍎 Appendix #1 🍎

The Qualitative Approach - A Case Study

How do I know that what I've written is true? Mainly by experience and observation. There isn't one assertion in this book that hasn't been confirmed, in myself and others, on many occasions. Chiefly, I know because I've been repeatedly duped or as I used to say, "swindled" by false approaches. I've already spoken about my struggles as a junior player, but quite recently I had a revelation about the shortcomings of all but the purely natural qualitative approach. This realization was prompted by my abysmal play at the provincial championships and it came as most intuitive incites do - like a flash of lightning, which hits you right between the eyes and makes you wonder how you could have missed what was so obvious! But to understand the story, we must go back a bit...

Three years ago. I sat on a committee that was revamping the ranking system for the Ontario Tennis Association. At the time, I was ranked number one in the open men's category, and one of the committee members used this fact to illustrate the inadequacy of the system. He remarked that while I was a good player it was inappropriate that I should be number one. At the time, I didn't object to this idea. On the contrary, I accepted it (though I did note his horrendous lack of tact in using that particular example in my presence).

After that I laboured under the influence of that *suggestion* about the quality of my tennis (recall, if you will, the section on the power of suggestion in chapter seven). Essentially, it shook my self-confidence; or to put it more accurately, my ability to let

NOBLE TENNIS
THE WISDOM OF SPORT

myself play as I can play, and know what I know. How did this work? Basically, since the time of that meeting built an *image* of myself as a player, based on the idea that while my successes, which have come largely within the confines of Eastern Ontario, and as a Varsity player, were perfectly appropriate within those contexts, I simply wasn't ready for the next level. This doubtful image arose just as I was preparing to play tournaments that included the whole scope of the province, and which counted towards national rankings. Accordingly, in the past three years, I've played three provincial championships and several other tournaments whose fields were bigger and stronger than where I played before. This was a natural progression. But my play at these events (which, not incidentally, were almost always run by the man who made the remark at the committee meeting) has been universally sub-standard. I've lost to players who were below my calibre, and blown considerable leads against others who were considered hot-shots in the country, but who, nevertheless, weren't really as good as I am. What's been going on? Clearly what's happened is that my self-created image, promoted by a cynical (even if innocent) suggestion, has dropped like a shadow between myself and the game. In a subtle and yet fully effective way, I've denied myself the victories that were clearly in my grasp, because a victory at that level would have contradicted the ideas I had tacitly accepted. Yes, suggestion is powerful stuff!

The above represents a qualitative, and therefore accurate account of what happened. But I didn't see it this way in the beginning. When I blew leads, I assumed that physical conditioning was responsible. I seemed to have "run out of gas." Also, I concluded that the quantity and/or quality of my technical training required upgrading. You may think this was a strange conclusion for the author of this particular book to have reached. Why didn't I look to the qualitative dimension? Well, the truth is, I did, but I didn't discriminate properly. When I looked at myself in terms of the five indispensable qualities, I saw no grave deficiency. The obvious signs of choking and nervousness, which were such a problem in my youth, weren't present, so I assumed it was merely a matter of physical deficiencies. Yes, it's so easy to reach for the physical diagnosis, especially when the psychological factors are a little more subtle than usual: in this case, a single comment made in a relatively distant past! Players usually find they have certain areas of recurring weakness. Mine has always been self-doubt, and a tendency to conform to the suggestions of others (suggestions which all-too-often support and confirm the doubting image). These weaknesses will show themselves in increasingly subtle ways as we master and leave behind their cruder and more obvious expressions. This was something I forgot.

How do you think, I should have responded to the realization that an alien suggestion had influenced me in such an unpleasant way? Conventional wisdom would allow me to blame my assailant; person X made a cruel comment, and it shook my self-esteem; he was mean and hurtful, and I've paid dearly for his unkindness. This, however, misses the central point and the central opportunity of the whole episode. Consider: if I had been in the zone, in the flow, in the Tao, such a comment would have washed over me like water. *The player who is in the zone has no "self-Image,"* and issues of confidence are non-existent in that place. A player who is in the zone simply IS, without ego, without ambition and fear, without "confidence" or the lack of it, they play the game - fully, completely, joyously; they have no thought of rankings, capacities, results, levels of play, provincial versus national versus varsity tennis, etc. Hence, the real question is this - what, *in me,* allowed the comment to have such an impact, and

NOBLE TENNIS
THE WISDOM OF SPORT

why didn't I notice what was happening, and address it immediately? What ambitions, expectations and insecurities were active in me, that I could have responded to an unhelpful idea with such zeal and obedience? Now the whole thing has changed don't you think? Suddenly, I'm essentially responsible and I can even thank the "mean man" (mentally) for providing me with an opportunity to make these realizations, which represent a qualitative achievement of great importance. For, indeed, the comment at the meeting had awakened in me a subtle ambition to prove that I really deserved to be number one in Ontario. This, of course, was disastrous, and was a direct breach of my own qualitative knowledge and principles. When I became aware of this, it allowed me, once again, to let go of fear and ambition, thereby entering further into joy.

Thus, the qualitative approach is powerful and effective. Sport, under its guidance, becomes a psychological adventure which is much like a murder mystery - the detective must observe, she must be vigilant and alert, she must understand what motivates herself and others, she must bypass obvious but inadequate explanations, and discover the true causes of things. These causes always make sense, and they explain everything. As Sherlock Holmes says, "ultimately, everything makes sense, and nothing is quite what it appears to be - all things have their hidden side."

🍎 Appendix #2 🍎

Competition and Cooperation: The Connection

Competition is valued very highly in the modern world. In practically everything - from economics to law to politics to sport - we see competition, the "adversarial system," as the path to efficiency, effectiveness, prosperity and greatness. But what is competition, really, and why is it valuable? Is it valuable? Does it bring about the things we think it does? Let's explore a little...

A competition is a contest. It's a situation in which one thing strives against another. In this process, all the resources of each competitor are called to the surface- strengths and weaknesses are revealed; intelligence, intuitiveness and skill are tested. Those who have the most strength, and the most refined qualities, win, while those who are lacking in some area are eliminated from the contest. They must continue to practice and improve, so they can do better the next time. A competition, in other words, is like a snapshot - it reveals where people stand at a given point in time.

A great competition has transforming effects. It's like rubbing two sticks together - the friction can become so great that both the sticks ignite, thereby producing the spectacle of fire. In this case, the wood has been transformed into something rare and unexpected - possibilities, unsuspected even by the sticks themselves, are released and revealed. If it weren't for the friction, the "competition," these higher possibilities would never have been evoked and discovered. Athletes can relate to this: in the heat of the contest, we discover resources and abilities that were hidden, and which could never have been demonstrated if the

NOBLE ◯ TENNIS
THE WISDOM OF SPORT

impetus of the competitive scenario hadn't been provided. Truly, the sticks cannot ignite if they never come together.

This idea of coming together introduces a whole new element to competition, and that is cooperation. Indeed, when we look closely we discover that cooperation is ninety per cent of competition! The great athlete is the one who achieves total cooperation with herself and her environment: internally, or psychologically, there is no friction between mind and body (no sport psychologist recommends that the ideal performance state will be reached when mind and body are at odds with one another!); and externally, the player is in harmony with their environment - they adapt, for instance, to the various elements, such as sun, wind, court surface, etc., thereby cooperating with the unique possibilities and circumstances that these factors introduce. Further, it's even true that every shot is really an act of cooperation - in reception we respond harmoniously and cooperatively to the characteristics of the ball, and in projection we cooperate with the laws of biomechanics (and, also, if we're smart, with the unspoken agreement between players that, in a competition, they will play to each other's weaknesses!).

These ideas are food for thought, but they are only the beginning: to reach their potential, players must cooperate with coaches, and coaches with players; and these, in turn, must work cooperatively with parent's, clubs, schools, organizers, provincial and national and international associations, the rules of the game, and so on. If cooperation is lacking on any of these fronts, the situation will be, at best, unpleasant, and perhaps even totally untenable.

Thus, sport is a cooperative enterprise, and competition is a cooperative contest, within a cooperative structure. I think this recognition could revolutionize our conception of competition, and help to remove the mean-spiritedness and hostility that it tends to evoke. These inhumane elements can and must be eliminated. Sport is meant to serve the growth and development of human beings, as human beings. A competition is simply an assessment period - a small step on the great, infinite, cooperative path of human perfectibility. Tournaments and competitions should be opportunities - times when people come together for purposes of appreciation, support, observation and striving. With such an attitude, we might even take seriously the old cliché, "it's not if you win or lose, it's how you play the game."

previously printed in "Ontario Tennis", the magazine of the Ontario Tennis Association, Summer, 1997.

🍎 Appendix #3: 🍎

The Dignity of Sport

In Ancient Greece, where the Olympics were born, sport was seen primarily as a means to an ethical end; the spirit of sport was identical with the spirit of goodwill and human dignity, and the competition, the contest, was subordinate to these values. In the Far East, sport was understood as a way to unfold the spiritual and moral capacities that lie latent in human nature. Thus, ethics have traditionally been central to sport. I wonder if that's really the case today?

Sport is a major force in the modern world. Millions and millions of people participate in thousands of athletic enterprises. As coaches who are involved in this world-wide activity, we have a responsibility to ensure that the influence of sport will be a constructive, harmless and uplifting one. Athletes, after all, are people, and it is people - their values, attitudes and modes of acting – who will dictate the future of this planet. Sport helps to define the characteristics of people, and therein lies its major challenge and opportunity.

Such a broad attitude towards sport is absolutely essential. Coaches, players and parents are easily distracted by ephemeral concerns over winning and losing, but how valuable is a top ranking, or a scholarship, or even a career, in a world that's falling apart because it has forgotten about the necessity of ethics and morality - that is, about principles of thinking and acting that ensure personal dignity and basic decency in all relationships?

NOBLE TENNIS
THE WISDOM OF SPORT

As a coach, citizen and player, I follow Immanuel Kant, the great German philosopher, who said that ethical laws and injunctions represent "categorical imperatives." This means that there's no "gray area" when it comes to morality. The "fair play philosophy" of an organization like Tennis Canada is the voice of basic, child-like conscience, but conscience is meaningless when partially obeyed.

Thus, the players that I coach understand, from the beginning, that while great patience will be shown with technical errors, tactical blunders and mental distractions, loud or abusive language, mistreatment of facilities or equipment, cheating, or gamesmanship of any kind, is simply not an option. This sounds simple, and it is, but it requires of both coach and player an understanding that there is no justification - competitive or personal - for such behaviors; there is, again, no "gray area," no circumstance under which such measures become appropriate. Thus, gamesmanship won't be returned with gamesmanship, nor cheating with cheating; and players are not permitted to seek out that fine line that runs between the spirit and the letter of the law - they must obey both.

All this makes perfect sense to younger kids, whose conscience is usually pure and unobscured. I have found that when I'm clear they follow along happily and without resistance. Indeed, they will be proud of their ethical principles, if you make it evident that such things represent the highest good and victory. Certain older players, and the odd young one, can be more difficult. Here, the coach must get to the root *causes* of the un-ethical behavior. These are almost always the same – fear, ambition and materialism.

NOBLE TENNIS
THE WISDOM OF SPORT

Modern society teaches that selfish, materialistic, competitive goals are "natural" and good. This ethos of egoism creates a bunker mentality - me against the world, with my loss being your gain, and vice-versa. The natural results or effects of such attitudes are fear [of failure primarily], paranoia, and a sense that "if I don't do it to you, you'll do it to me." Then, under the influence of such conceptions, we see the slippery slope from the purity of sport into the "gray"' of gamesmanship and the black of cheating. Meanwhile, ethics operate in just the opposite way - my gain is everyone's gain, and no one can defeat me, except myself.

Thus, when a coach commits him or herself to ethics and regards them as categorical, they are actually working towards a total rehabilitation of sport. The truest and greatest purpose of sport is in the full realization of our humanity, and immorality, being beneath human dignity, runs entirely counter to that aim. Coaches, therefore, must see through the momentary issues of the contest to the lasting impact of sport on individuals, communities and the world.

Previously printed in "Topspin", official newsletter of the Canadian Society of Tennis Teaching Professionals.

NOBLE TENNIS
THE WISDOM OF SPORT

NOBLE TENNIS

THE WISDOM OF SPORT

Try This! Summary

Chapter I

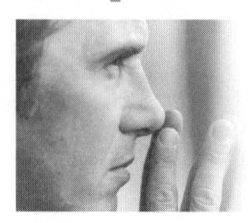

When scouting, look for people who are preoccupied with their sport in the absence of any coercion or outward incentives. For instance, the young tennis player: when faced with a choice, do they watch tennis? When all the courts at the club are booked, do they sneak into a squash court and play? Do they hit against the wall? Do they read tennis books and magazines? These are important indicators, which should be considered by parents as well as coaches. We must learn the difference between fleeting curiosity and deep enthusiasm.

Beware of the many pitfalls that can sap the purity of enthusiasm. At tournaments, for instance, stand aloof from the incessant speculation over results, rankings, etc. The sport is the source of joy, and the aim is to participate fully in the playing. Everything else is secondary, and follows naturally from this innocent absorption.

Avoid the temptation to consider athletics as an "investment" – that is, something from which some material or status-related benefit will come. These things may occur, but when these motivations replace enthusiasm, the situation is destructive and unwholesome. Parents, do you really wish to think of your children as corporations, and you a share-holder? Do you want to drive your child, like investors drive corporations, to seek

material profit at any cost, knowing that 'failure' will result in withdrawn support? Are you content being a fear-monger? Psychological well-being is the top priority. All the rest follows. Look for pure enthusiasm, and work with it. Applying this hint may require some inward de-programming. Observe your thoughts, words and deeds, and substitute vital, joyous enthusiasm for grasping, smothering desires.

Think and speak in terms of pure enthusiasm and rhythm. To quietly affirm the strength and rhythm of a heartbeat, or the flow of natural breathing, is to dissolve feelings of confusion and trepidation. There is no chaos there, and from within that space we can proceed naturally, purely, happily. Try it and see. Work with athletes to establish natural rhythms in both athletic and non-athletic settings. Sporadic patterns of sleep, for instance, will prove detrimental. Special emphasis should be placed on the natural rhythms before and, where applicable, between athletic exertions. Everything that enhances the feeling of natural rhythm is good, and there are many athletes who would benefit greatly from dance lessons, as also by hearing harmonious music. Think everywhere of rhythm – in eating, sleeping, playing. Pure enthusiasm leads to rhythm, and rhythm leads to everything else.

Observe enthusiasm levels. These levels are revealed by the overall atmosphere or "aura" of the player, plus posture, facial expression, speed of movement, etc. I sometimes ask students (usually at the beginning of a lesson) to rate their degree of enthusiasm between zero and ten. If it's less than ten, I ask why, *and we don't proceed until the issue is resolved. The resolution may require a discussion, whose aim is to re-kindle inspiration by reminding the student of their love for the game; it may mean canceling a practice, especially if the cause of the depressed energy is fatigue or illness; it may mean doing a favorite drill, one that releases the player into the flow of enthusiasm: If enthusiasm is lacking over a period of time, look to causes, which can range from lack of sleep to fear over results, and see if these can be addressed. Sometimes, a break from the game will be required. This should be considered part of training, since the maintenance of enthusiasm is the precondition of effective training.*

Seek for the third option that overcomes both "fooling around" and "drilling." Begin by seeking the proper attitude as you prepare to coach. Before addressing your athletes take a moment to look at and think of them as human beings, as miracles of nature with a vast potential. Can you feel the warmth and broadness of this understanding? Your students will pick it up subconsciously. Feel the responsibility that comes with influencing the growth and development of your fellows, and then proceed. You will demonstrate a synthesis of seriousness and lightness. You are serious about the work of developing human potential and passionate about the medium you have chosen, but you are also good natured. Your students will experience you as one who is more mature than they, detached and dignified and knowing, but also as a warm friend they can trust. This is the natural relation between teacher and student.

NOBLE TENNIS
THE WISDOM OF SPORT

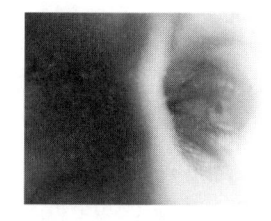

Make a list of the symptoms of stress and the features of happiness, as you have experienced and observed them. You might notice that they are often opposites. Record your observations as to what induces stress and what allows enthusiasm to remain pure. Note also what activities, words and thoughts are effective in eliminating stress and affirming happiness. This is simply being responsible for the well-being of oneself and one's students.

Study enthusiasm. Specify a certain period of time in which you will observe all things, such as patterns of sleeping, eating and thinking, in terms of their impact on enthusiasm. What releases and maintains a complete, fearless, active absorption in living, and what saps you of this ability? A log book can be maintained in which observations of oneself and others are recorded. Coaches and players can discuss and observe together. This will be very useful. We must become as seriously interested in the great, indispensable qualities as most of us are in other things, like the stock market.

Do not underestimate the power and significance of enthusiasm. Enthusiasm isn't just a quaint, childish, adorable feeling, nor is it a fleeting emotion. It's a fundamental energy, and it contains a fabulous intelligence. The ability to recognize and dismiss suggestions and activities, whether mental, verbal or physical, that disturb the purity of enthusiasm requires sincerity and vigilance. It will become a preoccupation for those who see and feel the significance of what is being said.

Chapter 2

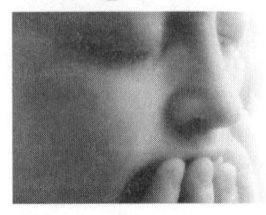

Make silence an integral aspect of life and training. The creation of a calm, fearless atmosphere is the primary responsibility of all. Silence should be introduced as an element of pre and post-match stretching, for instance. Soft music and deep breathing, combined with an emphasis on the rhythmic nature of the movements, will all be helpful in this regard. Trips to parks and gardens may also be useful. The serenity and beauty of nature are powerful ingredients in psychological health. Serenity can be maintained at all times, but familiarity with the feeling must first be attained.

One of the best ways to recover a lost sense of serenity is to simply listen to the natural rhythm of your heartbeat, or the inflow and outflow of breath. This returns us to natural simplicity and rhythm. However, as understanding is increased, a single thought will often prove sufficient. Thus, the more juvenile ideas and preoccupations can be dismissed as we say, "I am simply here to play." In this way, the self-created opera will be seen as silly, and the whole structure will dissolve before the power of an understanding smile. Eventually, not even words will be required, as our whole feeling about what we are doing and why can be re-oriented in silence. Silence and feeling are powerful.

NOBLE TENNIS
THE WISDOM OF SPORT

Constantly recommend serenity over analytic thought. If, during a match, nervousness begins to set in, begin by taking a few deep breaths. When the feeling of quiet has been restored, proceed. Practice this, perhaps with the aid of key phrases. With one student I recommended that he say, " I observe, I do not react." After serenity has been restored, observations and refinements can be made, but this will look and feel very different from the analytic control mania.

Remember that serenity is fully compatible with close observation. Test yourself or your students on their observational skills. See who notices little changes in the environment. Serenity creates an attentiveness that is totally free of fear and judgment. Analytic babble, like all forms of speculation, separates us from reality. Serenity, on the other hand, connects us with what is actually going on, and this has major implications in terms of rhythm and coordination. Serenity is like being in the flow of a river. The desire to get outside the river and control the flow is the big problem.

Practice non-judgment. Have practice sessions whose only theme is the complete absence of evaluation in terms of good and bad, right and wrong. Similarly, ask athletes to relate what they have observed during a match or a drill, or indeed in any context, and clarify when what they are offering is a judgment. For instance, if you ask for observations on a match and you hear

"I played like crap," realize that that's an evaluation, not an observation. In serenity, we observe and refine, we learn, and this is a totally different feeling from that of judging.

Recognize that serenity cannot be forced into existence. It comes when the lower nature, the site of fear and mental babbling, is quiet. Thus, our primary work is to address and eliminate the ideas and preoccupations that produce fear and analysis. This is an ongoing project, requiring observation and communication over time. I recommend discussions and activities whose theme is serenity, but, best of all, I recommend developing the alertness that notices opportunities as they arise. This alertness is born when the significance of serenity is recognized.

In the story of the "Tony turn-around" we see the essential outlines of a process that is universally applicable. First, there is silence, whose importance cannot be overstated. This is aided by a temporary feeling of detachment from the outward environment. Hence we see athletes putting towels over their heads, or just bowing their head downwards and looking at their shoelaces, or their racquet strings. We see similar rhythms of momentary abstraction in the regular routines of baseball pitchers, for instance, and many other examples could be furnished. It is the crucial process of isolating oneself from the worldly, with all its distractions and psychological snares, and uniting with an inward realm of serenity and strength. Thus, the position of the athlete could be called one of "isolated unity." From within the detached silence, there is no chaos, no noise, no clutter. All the rest follows. My "turn around"

included some words, and these embodied a thought that affirmed serenity. Such words may or may not be necessary. They normally won't be when the process is proceeding naturally – when the player is in the zone, but a supportive phrase will often prove useful when the athlete is struggling to regain a position of serenity. In all this there is no need for distinctly Pavlovian methods. The essential understanding and requirements need to be clarified and discussed and experienced, but it is best when the particulars are left to the spontaneous intelligence of the athlete. This makes of serenity something that is familiar and intimate and valuable. People can never feel this way when they are imposing a theory that comes from the outside.

During on-court sessions, address serenity as an aspect of efficiency and effectiveness. Is what you observe a technical or physical inability, or is it the result of tension? How can you know if it's a genuine technical problem when the cause may be purely inward? Would this still be a problem if there were suppleness and rhythm, which come with enthusiasm and serenity? Thus, when I stop a drill, it is often to ask, "who is playing here?" Is this enthusiasm and serenity in a process of learning, in which case we have a technical area to address, or not? Do not assume that your technical chatter is going to be useful when mental babbling and emotional turmoil are precisely the problems at hand. Also, observe bodily tension. A lack of tension in the mouth and jaws, combined with an almost "droopy" feeling around the eyes, are sure signs of serenity. Sometimes the simple action of relaxing a clenched jaw or letting the shoulders fall will be valuable as a first step on the road to calmness. Self-conscious tension must be addressed in all learning environments. The absence of calmness

cuts off all your natural rhythm and coordination, your instinctive intelligence, and makes learning almost impossible.

Employ serenity exercises, like deep breathing, as introductory aids. Even five minutes per day will be useful. All that really matters is the sense of familiarity with the feeling of serenity. The form of these exercises is not particularly important. You can count your breaths, up to ten and then start over, or just breath and be quiet, or just look attentively and appreciatively out a window! Make sure the posture is correct while doing any such work. I did this with one student who noted that the first few times five minutes felt like five hours, but it got easier and easier each day. Indeed, most people are sadly unfamiliar with the feeling of disciplined stillness. Ultimately, meditation can be undertaken on a busy street corner, and why not, for it is simply an attentive frame of mind.

Chapter 3

Develop the ability to notice irritation when it begins. Insensitivity allows little problems to develop into big problems. Irritation, unaddressed, overwhelms its victims. Thus, when practicing, do not let irritation flourish. Follow a three step procedure: 1) notice, 2) stop, get quiet, and 3) proceed, observe, learn, enjoy.

Realize that patience must be connected and united with enthusiasm and serenity. Patience without enthusiasm is ugly; it's a kind of suffering. And patience without serenity isn't patience at all, but the suppression of a time bomb. Patience as stubbornness and resentment must be removed. We replace these with patience as the great joy of constant learning, free from fear. Only when patience is based in enthusiasm and serenity can we affirm the old cliché which says that "patience is a virtue." The wise coach will stress patience because it alone ensures that lack of familiarity with sustained effort will not dampen enthusiasm or transform serenity into its opposite, its nemesis – irritation.

When doing drills or activities whose theme is patience, be sure to match the duration of the exercise to the experience of the student. Do drills that will definitely take them beyond their usual degree of patience, but do not carry the exercise to extremes that will harm the quality of the work, or lead to injury. We must be patient, even as we strive for patience, lest we end up

like the person who says, "Lord, grant me patience, and grant it to me right now!"

When taking on new students, assess patience levels and, where necessary, do drills or assign work that will test and enhance this quality. This may require a stated "preliminary" period, in which you learn whether or not the player is capable of being a student. It is perfectly acceptable to inform students of the purpose underlying this preliminary work.

Get used to using the language of the qualitative approach. Discuss tactical and technical elements in terms of patience. Let students experiment. Ask them to hit their usual serve, but to apply patience from start to finish. See what happens.

Chapter 4

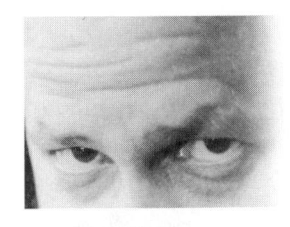

Have discussions where the true nature of concentration is considered. Concentration is so confused with violence and personal will that some clarification is badly needed.

Demonstrate the energy of concentration to yourself and your students. I have walked before whole groups of people and changed the entire atmosphere by becoming quiet, focused and powerful in their midst. They see and feel the collection of energy, the deep focused silence, the penetrating look, the deep joy and interest, the love of life and potential. This works well at the beginning of a lesson, or when groups of kids are getting too hyper, or if a team is nervous. Concentration is a transforming energy, and it creates a dynamic environment.

Never use fear or threats as spurs to concentration, and do not appeal to selfish ambition. These are the very energies that stifle the greater potential and happiness of the human being. The release of that potential is the fundamental concern, and it alone can provide sufficient motivation and reward. Therefore, stress what is humanly good and humanly possible, and the peculiar way that each will express these things. Make that the goal, and strive relentlessly in that direction. This is not a trifling distinction; it's a different space from which to work.

NOBLE ◉ TENNIS
THE WISDOM OF SPORT

Where concentration is deficient, deal with causes. Is it a lack of familiarity with sustained attention? Then work progressively in this area, through on and off-court exercises. Is it that fear and doubt are constantly causing the mind to wander? Then address fear. Is it a lack of enthusiasm? Then address that. The ability to recognize the source of any lack will grow through communication and experience.

Experiment with the "wait and see" progression. Make it a training theme for one month. Be vigilant, and employ it as required, while, at the same time, noticing the factors that separate us from this natural and effective way of being. All methods, however wonderful, are stop-gap measures. The real work is to remove the conditions that make the methods necessary.

Always begin exercises, such as counting breaths, with serenity, stressing that concentration is something we allow, not something we force. If concentration wanders, patiently re-affirm the serenity, and then proceed.

Introduce concentration as a way of being, a way of life, rather than a specialized skill that we apply only for the achievement of grandiose ambitions. Take the time to really look at a flower, to notice its shape, color and scent. Notice what players

notice, and what they do not notice, and begin the work of expanding their degree of interest and attentiveness. Rearrange the objects in a room and see who notices. This is crucial for noble coaching and parenting, which seeks the blossoming of people, not just players. The idea is to integrate the noble qualities as features of who we are. In this realm, one leads by example, and also by creating or pointing out opportunities for interest in fascinating things.

Chapter 5

Observe the workings of fear, and see whether it enhances harmony and intelligence, or whether it is their mortal enemy. The idea that fear is natural and valuable is very common, but is it right? Is the fear-fuelled world the best and only option we have? These are critical questions for sport, and for life.

It is wise to hold the phenomenon in the spotlight of the mind. Question your fears. Ask whether they are beneficial or not. We do that with almost everything else in life, so why not with psychological qualities? Write your fears down on paper – make them real, and then see if those fears can stand up to your reason and your courage. State alternatives to the fearful attitude and how an altered perspective will alter your actions and responses. These types of discussions can also take place in instructional settings, and if this means that the better part of a lesson is spent in discussion, do not regard it as something separate or superfluous. Many players and coaches think they're not teaching or learning if they aren't constantly "drilling," and parents often resent it when they see this "chit-chat" going on, but what's the use of all that physical work if fear can overtake you at any moment?

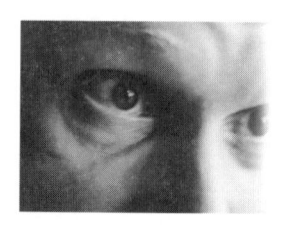

Discuss fear frequently. See how it functions. A deep recognition of the absurdity and folly of fear is a crucial and potent element on the path to fearlessness. Of course, you may reject fearlessness as

an option, but at least you'll be conscious of what you are doing and why. That's better than the "monkey see, monkey do" approach of most people today, who repeat cliches about fear without any reflection, and without any observation of their own experience.

Realize that the whole world can be divided between those who think fear is necessary and those who strive for fearlessness. The latter may be in the minority, but does that make them wrong? You must think and see for yourself. If you accept fear, then the wisdom of sport and the qualitative approach are not for you.

Chapter 6

Actively replace the thought "I want, so I play", with the thought "I am, and I play." Mantras like this are effective, and they can be developed or expanded in accordance with the intuition of each person. Fear begins with a thought that embodies a perspective. Change the thought and you change everything.

Make it clear that fear is the one thing that must not motivate our actions. Encourage players to become sensitive to the types of environment that promote fear, such as tournaments, and the types of thought that act as trigger mechanisms for the onset of fear. Remind student's that they can respond to the first whiff of fear. Do not pretend it's not there, thereby allowing it to grow and develop to bigger and bigger proportions. Fear motivation can be replaced with motivation by interest.

Discuss the attitude that revels in freedom from the snares of competitiveness and materialism. Perhaps watch films or read books about great heroes who have lived free from the pettiness and fear that these preoccupations breed. The film "Chariots of Fire" is brilliant in this respect. Eric Liddel represents the free man, while Harold Abrams represents the one who is struggling with ambition, pride and fear. Also, I would recommend the films "Little Buddha," "Phenomenon" and "Searching for Bobby Fisher."

NOBLE TENNIS
THE WISDOM OF SPORT

It is crucial that people discover people by whom they can be inspired to fearlessness, and who point to the truly significant thing, which is human potential.

Realize that fearlessness is evolved in and through living relationships. Life itself presents opportunities to address fear. We cannot do it artificially. Our task is to understand fear and fearlessness, and to apply this understanding in life. Thus, fearlessness must become an important theme in your thinking and observing. When this occurs, it will cross your mind to deal with things at this level, and you will become vigilant, sensitive and effective.

Make experiments. Go to a tournament and make fearlessness via solemnity, humor or applied knowledge the sole or dominant theme. Later, this can be branched out, and the player can intuit which of these responses is most apt. Eventually, this artificiality will not be necessary at all. We must remember that fearlessness is possible, so the need for antidotes indicates incomplete attainment. Fear is something we leave behind; we forget about it. This forgetting cannot occur if we are unduly preoccupied with battling fear as a problem. The emphasis needs to be on enthusiasm and serenity. That way, fear will be something we notice, but not something we actively attract. The work of replacing "I want" with "I am" represents the creation of an environment that does not attract, or produce, fear.

Chapter 7

Take seriously the Tennis Canada injunction to observe the psychological first. Practice this. Most coaches simply lack comfort and familiarity with the psychological life, so the technical and tactical win by default. However with knowledge of the indispensable qualities herein outlined, the situation can change. There is no excuse now, and continued neglect of the critical issues at hand will be the result strictly of laziness, habit, and prejudice.

Play practice matches during which the player, at change-overs, has to define what has occurred at the level of thought. They may find this difficult in the beginning. They will be inclined to tell you what physically happened, but this isn't really what you're after. Thus, you will need to clarify that what you're asking is if any thoughts or ideas occurred to them as they played, keeping in mind that the observation of total mental silence is perfectly valid, though quite unusual.

Keep a log of psychological observations and experiences. Don't rely on so-called experts – perform your own experiments! You are the experiment, and the experimenter.

NOBLE ⊙ TENNIS
THE WISDOM OF SPORT

Do exercises of mindfulness. For instance, try to go through one full day, or perhaps one hour, with a complete sense of what you are doing and why. Imagine – a day in full-waking consciousness, with little or no mental automatism, or merely conditioned routine.

Further exercises in mindfulness: say a "mantra" or phrase before each point; have players call out ball characteristics or appropriate shot selections during drills; ask questions to see who notices different things in the environment. True, all of this unnecessary in the zone, but the concentration of mindfulness is the spring-board that takes us there. It is preparatory work.

Endeavour to root out the unspoken assumptions and ideas that motivate players, and then examine whether they are constructive or not. This occurs easily when you ask questions – especially that master of all questions: why?, listen, and clarify the ideas that are being expressed. This can occur in off-court discussions, or it can be ignited by on-court situations, as they arise.

Get to know the three varieties or aspects of mind. What mind generally defines you? Which are you using now? Are you an isolated individual, fighting to get what you want? Are you a walking brain – an analyzing machine? Or are you an

193

NOBLE TENNIS
THE WISDOM OF SPORT

intelligence that's connected with a Greater Intelligence, one that has meaning and purpose in and of itself? When you meet a person, a new student perhaps, observe what kind of mind they bring. Make experiments. Run three practices, using the three different varieties of mind as the guiding principle. Note the responses of yourself and your students. Recall, when doing this, that the "I want" mind appeals to selfish ambition, will use fear as a motivator, and gets everyone "pumped!" The technical mind appeals to the sense of prudence and systematic method. The Creative mind brings an intense, calm strength and joy, plus a passion for life and sport. It is intensely observant, open, and contains an element that the other two minds tend to lack – humour. I suggest that the individualistic and technical aspects of mind only function properly when under the influence of the Creative. This Creative mind is synonymous with the zone, and is hence the critical factor in both practice and competitive settings. But what is anything I say? It's for you to try, and see.

In all your coaching and parenting, encourage and applaud insight, observation, and understanding. Demonstrate and encourage fine and noble feelings. Teach kids to revel in the playing of the game, and in the striving to mastery. This expansion of understanding and refinement of feeling is what it means to be a living, growing, maturing human being. We are not computers or slabs of meat to be simply "trained" and "drilled" and "programmed." If you can feel and know this, then you are on the path of noble tennis.

Chapter 8

Create an atmosphere of incessant learning. Address the attitude or mindset that is appropriate to physical training, thereby avoiding a lot of frustration and failure. Ask questions of your students and ensure that they have learned not just what to do, but how to do it, why they do it, why it works, why it makes sense, etc. There is a trinity of learning, practicing and observing. This is much better than the rival trinity of being told, remembering, and drilling.

Replace "drills we are going to do" with "things we are going to learn," or "things we are going to practice."

Keep a log of useful images and metaphors that apply to different strokes or situations. This log could also include a listing of the qualitative aspects of various physical/technical elements.

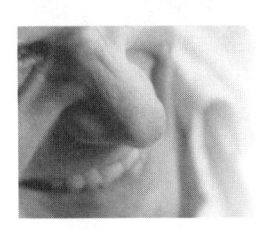

Incorporate rhythm as a central theme at all levels of playing and teaching. Explain, for instance, that the primary purpose of the warm-up is to establish a light or slow rhythm, which can then be increased. Address rhythm whenever necessary, before launching into a million technical observations. Do exercises

whose theme is the ability to respond to or create different tempos, and include rhythmic exercises, perhaps even dance lessons, as part of off-court training. Play music when playing (I've found a Strauss waltz can be quite effective), and always remember: tennis is a fore of dance.

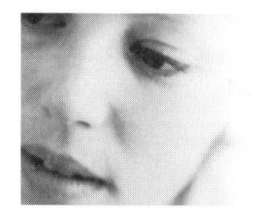

As you observe the barrage of technological advances in the realm of physical training and nutrition, ask yourself what is necessary, what is essential, and what is not. Are you being sucked into a preoccupation with things that don't really effect the ultimate purpose of sport – the growth and development of human beings, as human beings, and the attainment of the creative zone?

Try to arrange for physical fitness to emerge as an effect of useful activity. If this seems impossible, try at least to do fitness in beautiful, outdoor, natural settings.

Replace "stretching" with "yoga," recalling that suppleness and rhythm are the prerequisites of great tennis.

NOBLE TENNIS
THE WISDOM OF SPORT

Seek always to discover and import aspects of quality and meaning into physical training. The infusion of quality into the realm of quantity is our central task.

Chapter 9

See if you can eliminate all traces of aggression and hostility from the way you speak about sport in its psychological, physical, tactical and technical aspects. This will be a natural tendency when you change your thoughts about the game, and the spirit behind words is more important than the words themselves, but finding new terminology takes some conscious effort. For instance, I have replaced the idea of a "forcing" shot with that of a "building" shot. Eventually, I hope to arrive at a whole new vocabulary for tennis, based on harmony as the keynote. All contributions to this task will be greatly appreciated.

Revive in yourself and in your students/children the ideal of the honorable sportsman, the noble amateur. This is a worthy ideal, one that allows for the development of potential without the ugliness that surrounds athletics today. Speak of these things; teach the rules of sportsmanship and applaud their expression; create scenarios to practice responding with dignity and intelligence – and sometimes with indignation – to improper conduct. Make it real!

NOBLE TENNIS
THE WISDOM OF SPORT

If you travel with athletes, be it to a nearby city or around the world, insist that the travel include elements of cultural discovery and educational enlargement. Always, always stress and reveal the bigger picture. This will improve inward and outward health, as well as athletic "performance."

If you elect to do a goal-setting program, I recommend a three-tiered system. You will need three sheets of paper. On the first sheet are listed the goals. On the second sheet are listed the qualitative and quantitative aspects that are relevant to the meeting of the goal. These should be quite specific, for they will be assessed each day with a mark out of ten, based on the extent to which that quality or activity was carried through. The third sheet is a graph which lists the days of the month on the top and the numbered qualities and/or activities on sheet number two. It is here that marks are recorded. As a youngster, I found this organization helpful and efficient.

Biography

Tony Roth is a graduate of Queen's University, Kingston, Ontario, where he obtained an M.A. in philosophy. He has been teaching tennis for thirteen years, and is one of the most highly certified coaches in the country. He was recently named a National Touring Coach by Tennis Canada. he is also an accomplished player, having been ranked number one in his Province in the Open Men's category. Tony is currently the Tennis Director at the Kingston Tennis Club and Head Professional at the Landings Racquets and Fitness Club.